LUCA SIGNORELLI • CRUTTWELL, MAUD

PAGE
List of Illustrations ix 0

Bibliography xiii 0

Genealogical Tree xv 0

Chapter I. His Life 1 3

II. Development and Characteristics Of His Genius 17 8

III. Earliest Works 32 11

IV. Middle Period 49 17

V. Orvieto 63 21

VI. Later Paintings 87 29

VII. Last Works 98 32

VIII. Drawings 107 34

IX. Pupils and General Influence 11136

Chronological Table 121 38

Catalogue of Works 131 40

Index 141 43

[Pg ix]

LIST OF ILLUSTRATIONS
PAGE
Portrait of a Man *Gallery, Berlin* Frontispiece 2

Portrait of Signorelli *Museo del Duomo, Orveto* 8 5

The Deposition *Cathedral, Cortona* 10 5

The Flagellation *Brera Gallery, Milan* 32 11

Apostles *Santa Casa, Loreto* 34 12

The Incredulity of S. Thomas *Santa Casa, Loreto* 36 13

The Conversion of Saul *Santa Casa, Loreto* 36 13

Madonna and Saints *Cathedral, Perugia* 38 14

The Circumcision *National Gallery, London* 40 14

Pan *Gallery, Berlin* 42 15

Madonna *Uffizi, Florence* 44 15

Madonna and Saints *Pitti, Florence* 46 16

Holy Family *Rospigliosi Gallery, Rome* 46 16

Holy Family *Uffizi, Florence* 48 16

The Annunciation *Cathedral, Volterra* 50 17

[Pg x]
The Annunciation *Uffizi, Florence* 52 18

The Crucifixion *Santo Spirito, Urbino* 54 18

Miracle of S. Benedict *Monte Oliveto* 56 19

Miracle of S. Benedict *Monte Oliveto* 58 20

Saints *Gallery, Berlin* 60 20

Holy Family *Gallery, Berlin* 60 21

The Crucifixion *Municipio, Borgo San Sepolero* 62 21

Portraits of Signorelli and Fra Angelico *Cathedral, Orvieto* 64 22

Patriarchs *Cathedral, Orvieto* 68 23

The Preaching and Fall of Antichrist *Cathedral, Orvieto* 70 24

The Crowning of the Elect *Cathedral, Orvieto* 72 24

Subjects from Dante *Cathedral, Orvieto* 74 25

Heaven *Cathedral, Orvieto* 76 25

Hell *Cathedral, Orvieto* 76 25

The Damnation *Cathedral, Orvieto* 78 26

The Resurrection *Cathedral, Orvieto* 80 27

Signs of Destruction *Cathedral, Orvieto* 82 28

Madonna and Saints *Brera, Milan* 9030

Dead Christ upheld by Angels *S. Niccolò, Cortona* 92 30

The Adoration of the Magi *Jarvis Collection, [Pg xi] New Haven, U.S.A.* 94 31

Madonna and Saints *Mancini Collection, Città di Castello* 98 32

The Deposition *Santa Croce, Umbertide* 100 33

Madonna, Saints, and Prophets *Gallery, Arezzo* 102 33

Study of Nude Figure *Louvre, Paris* 108 35

Magdalen at the Foot of the Cross *Academy, Florence* 111 35

Tiberius Gracchus *Gallery, Buda-Pesth* 116 37

[Pg xii]

ERRATUM

Page 6 line 1, *for* "Pius II." *read* "Sixtus IV."

The Frontispiece and the illustrations facing pp. 40, 42, and 60 (2) are from photographs by Hanfstaengl (Munich), those facing pp. 46 (No. 2) and 68 by Anderson (Rome), that facing page 108 by A. Braun & Co. (Dornach and Paris), those facing pp. 94 and 116 from private photographs, and the remainder by Alinari (Florence).

[Pg xiii]

BIBLIOGRAPHY.

Luca Signorelli. Vasari, con annotazione di Gaetano Milanesi. (Firenze, G. C. Sansoni, 1879.) Vol. iii.

Luca Signorelli und die Italienische Renaissance. Robert Vischer. (Leipzig, 1879.)

Luca Signorelli. Cavalcaselle e Crowe. (Le Monnier, 1898.) Vol. viii.

Über Leben, Wirken und Werke der Maler Andrea Mantegna und Luca Signorelli. G. F. Waagen. (Historisches Taschenbuch von Raumer.)

Luca Signorelli. Manni. (Racolta Milanese di vari opuscoli, 1756.) Vol. i.

Storia del Duomo di Orvieto. Padre della Valle, 1791.

Il Duomo di Orvieto. Ludovico Luzi, 1866.

Memorie Ecclesiastiche e civili di Città di Castello. Muzi, 1844.

Istruzione Storico. Giacomo Mancini, 1832.

Notizie ... sopra Luca Signorelli. Girolamo Mancini, 1867.

Guida dei Monumenti ... nella provincia dell'Umbria, Guardabassi. 1872.

FAMILY TREE OF THE SIGNORELLI FAMILY.

Ventura di Signorelli.

Luca.

Egidio = A sister of Lazzaro dei Taldi (great-grandfather of Giorgio Vasari, the biographer).

Ventura. LUCA = Galizia Carnesecca.

Polidoro (Painter and Builder). Antonio = 1. Nannina di Paolo di Forzore. Pier Tommaso = Margherita di Vagnozzi. Gabriella = Mariotto del Mazza. Felicia = Luca della Bioscia.
2. Mattea di Domenico di Simone. Bernardina.

Lucrezia = Domenico di Gilio (Banker.) Francesco (Painter). = Felice Carrari. Rosata = Mariotto di Felice Passerini. Giulio. Filiziano.

Publisher's Note

Purchase of this book entitles you to a free trial membership in the publisher's book club at www.rarebooksclub.com. (Time limited offer.) Simply enter the barcode number from the back cover onto the membership form on our home page. The book club entitles you to select from millions of books at no additional charge. You can also download a digital copy of this and related books to read on the go. Simply enter the title or subject onto the search form to find them.

Note: This is an historic book. Pages numbers, where present in the text, refer to the first edition of the book and may also be in indexes.

If you have any questions, could you please be so kind as to consult our Frequently Asked Questions page at www.rarebooksclub.com/faqs.cfm? You are also welcome to contact us there.
Publisher: Books LLC™, Memphis, TN, USA, 2012. ISBN: 9781153807166.
Proofreading: pgdp.net

❈❈ ❈❈ ❈❈ ❈❈ ❈❈ ❈❈ ❈❈ ❈❈

Portrait of an unknown man
The Great Masters
 in Painting and Sculpture
 Edited by G. C. Williamson

LUCA SIGNORELLI

THE GREAT MASTERS IN PAINTING AND SCULPTURE.

The following Volumes have been issued

BERNARDINO LUINI. By George C. Williamson, Litt.D., Editor of the Series.

VELASQUEZ. By R. A. M. Stevenson.

ANDREA DEL SARTO. By H. Guinness.

LUCA SIGNORELLI. By Maud Cruttwell. — *December 1.*

RAPHAEL. By H. Strachey. — *January 1.*

In preparation.

CARLO CRIVELLI. By G. M'Neil Rushforth, M.A., Lecturer in Classics, Oriel College, Oxford.

CORREGGIO. By Selwyn Brinton, M.A., Author of "The Renaissance in Italian Art."

FRA ANGELICO. By Langton Douglas, M.A.

THE BROTHERS BELLINI. By S. Arthur Strong, M.A., Librarian to the House of Lords.

MICHAEL ANGELO. By Charles Holroyd, Keeper of the National Gallery of British Art.

TURNER. By Charles Francis Bell, M.A., Deputy Keeper of the Ashmolean

Museum.
PERUGINO. By G. C. Williamson, Litt.D., Editor of the Series.
MEMLINC. By W. H. James Weale, late Keeper of the National Art Library.
MURILLO. By Manuel B. Cossio, Litt.D., Ph. D., Director of the Musee Pedagogique, Madrid.
REMBRANDT. By Malcolm Bell.
Others to follow.
LONDON: GEORGE BELL & SONS

LUCA SIGNORELLI

BY

MAUD CRUTTWELL

LONDON
GEORGE BELL & SONS
1899

"Pianga Cortona omai, vestasi oscura,
Che estinti son del Signorello i lumi;
Et, tu, Pittura, fa de gli occhi fuimi,
Che resti senza lui debile e scura."
Epitaph composed at the time of his death
"Il Cortonese Luca d'ingegno
E spirito pellegrino."
Rime Di Giovanni Santi

PREFATORY NOTICE.

The references to Vasari, and Crowe and Cavalcaselle, are invariably to the latest editions, both in Italian: "Opere di Giorgio Vasari" (Firenze, G. C. Sansoni, 1879); "Cavalcaselle e Crowe" (Le Monnier, 1898).

The author desires to express her gratitude to Mr Bernhard Berensen, author of "Lorenzo Lotto," etc., for much help in her work.

Florence, *October* 1899.

[Pg vii]

[Pg 1]

LUCA SIGNORELLI

CHAPTER I

HIS LIFE

(BORN 1441: DIED 1523)

It is a curious fact that, considering the number of documents which exist relating to Signorelli, and the paintings time has spared, so little should be known beyond the merest outline of his life. The very dates of his birth and death are indirectly acquired; the documents leave his youth and early manhood an absolute blank, and there are only two of his numerous works which can with certainty be placed before his thirty-third year.
[1] 7
We are, therefore, forced to fall back upon traditional record, and by the aid of his biographer Vasari, and the evidence of youthful studies which his paintings contain, to patch together a probable account of his life, up to the time when the documents begin. On Vasari, in this case, we can depend with a certain amount of confidence, since Signorelli was his kinsman, and they had been in such personal communication as was possible between an old man and a child. [Pg 2]
From Vasari, then, we learn that Luca was born in Cortona, of Egidio Signorelli, and a sister of Lazzaro dè Taldi.

[2] 7
This Lazzaro, great grandfather of the biographer, deserves special mention, since it was through his means, and under his guardianship, that Luca was placed as a child to study painting with Pier dei Franceschi, at Arezzo.
[3] 7
Vasari tells us that Lazzaro was "a famous painter of his time, not only in his own country, but throughout Tuscany, with a style of painting hardly to be distinguished from that of his great friend, Pietro della Francesca."
[4] 7
This, however, is an assertion that has never been supported, and was probably based on the author's pride in his own family, for in the Cortona tax-receipts for the year 1427, he is described merely as a harness-maker (*Sellajo di Cavalli.*)
[5] 7
There is, besides, no record of him among the painters of Arezzo, and no fragment remains of the many works enumerated by his great-grandson. But it is of little consequence whether he was a painter of pictures or a decorator of saddles; what is to our purpose is the fact, that by his means Luca was placed under the tutelage of the painter most capable of developing the noblest qualities of his genius.

Luca was born about 1441, as we gather from Vasari, and if 1452 is the correct date of his uncle Lazzaro's death, his apprenticeship to Pier dei Franceschi must have begun before his eleventh year. It is probable [Pg 3] that, with his fellow-pupil Melozzo da Forlì, his senior by three years, Signorelli assisted the master with the frescoes in S. Francesco, although there is no trace of any work that might be from his hand. Vasari tells us that as a youth he laboured "to imitate the style of his master," with such success, that (as he remarked of Lazzaro) their work was hardly to be distinguished apart."
[6] 7
The nearest approach to the style of Piero that remains to us is "The Flagellation," of the Brera, Milan, which, however, already shows signs of a more deeply impressed technical influence, but it was probably under Piero's training that Signorelli developed his broad methods of work, and the grand manner which makes his painting so impressive. The later influence visible in the above-mentioned "Flagellation," as throughout all his work, is that of Antonio Pollaiuolo. To him and to Donatello are due the most important features in his artistic development, and in technique he follows much more readily than the Umbrian, the Florentine methods, with which his painting has nearly everything in common. Of the influence of Donatello it may justly be said that every painter and sculptor of the fifteenth century submitted to it, but few were so completely touched by his spirit as Signorelli. Not only, as we shall see

later, did he transfer attitudes and features from Donatello's statues into his earlier paintings, but he caught, and even exaggerated, the confident and somewhat arrogant spirit of his work, and exploited it with the same uncompromising realism.

The influence of Antonio Pollaiuolo was still more important, and is so evident in the whole mass of his [Pg 4] painting, that with no other warrant we may feel certain that he spent a considerable time either as pupil or assistant to the Florentine master. The passion of Pollaiuolo was to discover the science of movement in the human frame. "He understood the nude in a more modern way than the masters before him," says Vasari, "and he removed the skin from many corpses to see the anatomy beneath."

[7] 7

He was, in fact, the great anatomical student among the Quattrocento artists; and, having the same tastes, it was natural that to his workshop Signorelli should turn, in order to satisfy his own craving for knowledge of the structure of bones and muscles. The internal evidence of his paintings warrants this supposition, but there is no record of any residence in Florence, beyond the announcement of Vasari, that he went there after his visit to Siena, not at all as a student, but as a fully-fledged painter, making gifts of his pictures to his friend and patron, Lorenzo dei Medici. His work, however, proves so incontestably the training of Pollaiuolo, and shows so close an acquaintance with Florentine works of art, that we may safely presume the greater part of his youth, after leaving the studio of Pier dei Franceschi, to have been passed in Florence as pupil or assistant of Antonio.

It is a wide leap from these days of study to the beginning of his citizen's life in Cortona, when, a man of thirty-eight, he first settled down as a burgher discharging important duties there, but it would be idle to attempt to fill the gap, and only one document exists to help in any way to bridge it over. This is a commission from the Commune of Città di Castello, dated [Pg 5] 1474,

[8] 7

requiring Signorelli to paint, over some older frescoes in their Tower, a large "Madonna and Saints," but, unfortunately the work itself no longer exists, for what time and neglect had spared, the earthquake of 1789 completely destroyed. We may presume that before 1479 he painted the important frescoes for the Church of the Holy House at Loreto, since in that year he was first appointed to the municipal offices in Cortona, which necessitated an almost constant residence there for the next three years, as the documents of election show.

[9] 7

These numerous papers (for the most part discovered through the efforts of Signor Girolamo Mancini, and published in his "Notizie"), are preserved in the archives of Cortona, and form the chief evidence of the painter's whereabouts up to the end of his long life. They record, first, his appointment in the autumn of 1479 to the Council of XVIII., and to the Conservatori degli Ordinamente,

[10] 7

in the following spring to the Priori, and in the summer to the General Council, and they continue with few interruptions up to the very day of his death. They decide for us the social status he enjoyed, for both Priori and Councillors were chosen from the richest and most influential families, although not necessarily noble.

[11] 7

His official life began in a time of tumult and bloodshed. It was the year after the failure of the Pazzi Conspiracy, and all around Cortona [Pg 6] were pitched the camps of the rival troops of Sixtus IV. and the excommunicated Florentines. Cortona itself, as a frontier town of the Medici, was in the very centre of the fray; and besides these more important quarrels, there were the incessant internal bickerings between the nobles and the populace, which at that time divided every Italian city against itself. Altogether, the position of Magistrate in such a town, at such a time, could have been no sinecure, and it is difficult to understand how the hard-working painter could have found time or inclination to accept the citizen's duties, which were so weighty an occupation in themselves.

Much time has been spent in the vain search for documents relating to Signorelli's supposed visit, in 1484, to Rome, where, it is said, he was summoned to paint, with Perugino, Pintorricchio, Botticelli, and Cosimo Rosselli, the walls of the Sistine Chapel. Later criticism has perhaps accounted for the absence of such a record. Of the two frescoes there, formerly attributed to him, it is now no longer doubted that one—"The Journey of Moses and Zipporah"—is by Pintorricchio, and the opinion is gradually gaining ground that the other—"The Death of Moses"—although much nearer to Signorelli's style, is not sufficiently so as to permit us to accept it as his work.

[12] 7

[Pg 7]

The notices of the next few years contain little of interest beyond the facts, that in 1484 Signorelli painted the altarpiece in the Perugia Cathedral, the first dated picture remaining, and that in 1488 he received the much-coveted honour of citizenship from Città di Castello, for the "great ability" with which he painted a standard for the brotherhood of the Blessed Virgin,

[13] 7

a work which no longer exists. Soon after follows a document dated 1491, which bears witness that Luca had been invited by the authorities of Santa Maria dei Fiori in Florence to assist in judging the models and designs for the projected façade of that church.

[14] 7

This is important as a proof of the high esteem in which he was held in Florence, implying also that he must have understood something of architecture. He declined the invitation, perhaps for the same reason for which he had excused himself the month before from serving as Priore in his native town, "being absent at a distance of over forty miles,"

[15] 7

probably at Volterra. He painted there in this year three pictures, all of which are still in the city; the "Annunciation" and the "Madonna and Saints," dated 1491, and the fresco of "S. Jerome" on the walls of the Municipio.

The next notice of importance is of the year 1497, when he received the commission from the monks of S. Benedict to fresco the walls of their cloister at Monte Oliveto.

[16] 7

Here he painted eight episodes from the life [Pg 8] of the patron saint, leaving the rest of the work to be completed by Sodoma. Notwithstanding this task he found time, for four months of this very year, to serve among the Priori in Cortona, and accepted, besides, a fresh appointment as one of the Revisori degli Argenti.

In the following year he was in Siena, where he painted the altar-piece for the Bicchi family, the wings of which are now in Berlin.

[*Museo del Duomo, Orvieto*
PORTRAIT OF SIGNORELLI

We have now reached the most important time in Signorelli's life, the year in which he received the commission for the decoration of the Cappella Nuova in the Cathedral of Orvieto. Fifty years before, the roof had been begun by Fra Angelico, and ever since he went away, leaving it unfinished, the authorities had been undecided to whom to give the important work. Benozzo Gozzoli had begged for it; Perugino, it is said, had refused it; and now, in 1499, perhaps influenced to the choice by the success of the Monte Oliveto frescoes, they entrusted the work to Signorelli. Wishing first, however, to test his powers, they limited the commission to the completion of the vaulting, and it was not till the following year that they handed over to him the rest of the chapel, to be painted with the story of the Last Judgment. With this dramatic subject, and in these great spaces of the walls he had for the first time a free field for the wide sweep of his brush, and the force of his vivid imagination. The conceptions of Dante inspired, but did not trammel him, and he had sufficient strength to make the great drama his own, and to compel it to serve his ends in the display of the human frame in its most vigorous aspects. The portrait he has painted of himself in the first of the frescoes, as well [Pg 9] as that in the Opera del Duomo, show us a man in the very prime of life, full of energy and determination.

Four years at least, Signorelli laboured at these frescoes, although not consecutively, as we shall presently see. He had with him as assistant his son Polidoro,

[17] 7

and perhaps Girolamo Genga, and other pupils. He was apparently on friendly terms with the authorities, of one of whom, the treasurer Niccolò Francesco, he painted a portrait, side by side with his own above mentioned. It is on a brick or tile, on the back of which is a flattering inscription, evidently composed by Niccolò himself, in which he speaks of Signorelli as "worthy of comparison with Apelles."

[18] 7

Yet, notwithstanding this friendship with the treasurer, he could not get the money due to him, and it required the intervention of no less a person than Guidobaldo of Urbino, in 1506, to obtain it for him. A letter from the Prince is preserved in the Orvieto archives,

[19] 7

in which he writes: "Loving Maestro Luca di Cortona as I do, in no common measure, for his ability and rare talents, I can refuse him no possible favour in all that he may require of me," and goes on to beg the authorities for their love to him, to pay their debt to the painter, "which assuredly will be to me the greatest favour."

[*Cathedral, Cortona*
THE DEPOSITION

Even in fulfilling so arduous an undertaking as these great frescoes Luca did not abandon his magistrate's [Pg 10] work in his own city, and during the time, was serving both on the General Council and as one of the Priori. In 1502, moreover, he found time to paint for his Cathedral at Cortona the beautiful "Deposition," in which is a repetition of the Pietà of the Capella Nuova. The realism and pathos of this dead Christ are so convincing as to have given rise to the legend that it was painted from the body of his son, who died, or was killed, in this year. Vasari thus relates the incident: Luca had a son, "beautiful in face and person, whom he loved most dearly," killed in Cortona, whereupon, "overwhelmed with grief as he was, he had the body stripped, and with the greatest fortitude of soul, without tears or lamentation, he made a drawing of it, in order to have always before his eyes . what Nature had given him, and cruel Fate had snatched away."

[20] 7

This son, Antonio, probably a painter also, must have been a man of mature years at the time of his death, for he was already married to a second wife. The story has taken hold of the fancy of Signorelli's biographers, in the dearth of personal matter, and is the best known incident in his life, but it is more than probable that Antonio was carried off by the plague which, following close on the heels of the war of 1502, attacked Cortona, in which case it becomes a mere legend. We learn from a document, dated June 23rd, that the painter's house was not spared, for he excused himself from serving as Priore in that month, because the *peste bubbonica* had broken out in his family.

Four years later, Polidoro, his eldest son, and his assistant at Orvieto, died also. This happened while [Pg 11] Signorelli was on a visit to Siena, for it was there he bought the mourning cloth. The object of this visit was to design one of the subjects for the famous pavement of the Cathedral, but whether he ever did it we do not know; certainly it was never executed in marble.

In the next year we have the usual records of official appointments, and as a proof of his artistic activity, the two pictures still remaining in the little town of Arcevia, dated 1507 and 1508, one of them, the splendid *Ancona*, being among his finest works.

Now a man of nearly seventy, Signorelli's energies seemed to grow greater with increasing age, for in 1508 we find him, besides being elected to his usual offices, deputed as ambassador to Florence, to demand there permission to reform the offices and ordinances of Cortona, and in the same year he was at Rome, together with Perugino, Pintorricchio, and Sodoma, working at the decoration of the Vatican Chambers, already begun by Pier dei Franceschi. Giambattista Caporali gives a glimpse into their social life in Rome, telling of a supper given in their honour by Bramante [21]—Bramante, to whose introduction to the Pope of the young Raffaelle it is due that none of their work, with the exception of Perugino's ceiling, remains to us. How much Signorelli painted we do not know. Vasari says, "He had successfully completed one wall," [22] but so enchanted was Julius II. with the [Pg 12] facile and modern style of Raffaelle, that after he had finished the "Stanza della Segnatura," he forced him to destroy the paintings of the older masters and delivered the entire work to him and his assistants: a caprice which points a very significant turn in the history of painting—the triumph of the late Renaissance over the giants of the past.

Signorelli seemed destined to find nothing but disappointment in Rome. Five years later, an old man of seventy-two, he again went there, this time on the accession of Giovanni dei Medici, in 1513, to the Papal chair. Knowing the luxurious nature of the new Pope, and remembering the intense passion of his father Lorenzo for art and letters, to Rome flocked poets and painters, sculptors and architects, from every part of Italy, in the hope of work or of reward, and among them came Signorelli, with reasonable expectation of employment, and notice from the son of his old patron and friend. [23] Like his predecessor, however, Leo X. preferred the more modern school of Raffaelle and his pupils, and Luca had to return disappointed to Cortona. In connection with the visit exists a curious document, which has smirched too long the honour of the painter. It is the famous letter of Michelangelo, preserved among [Pg 13] the Buonarotti archives, in which he makes a complaint to the Capitano of Cortona, that Signorelli, sick with the ingratitude of the Medici "for the love of whom he would have had his head cut off," had borrowed of him eighty *juli* with which to return to Cortona; that on application for the money, Luca declared it to have been already repaid, so that now he—Michelangelo—sees no other way of obtaining his own but by application to the Capitano for justice. [24] This is the gist of the letter; we have to use our own knowledge of the character of the two men to decipher the mystery, since no other document confirms or denies the accusation. The reasonable explanation seems to be that some delay, probably on the road, in the transmission of the money, irritated the notoriously impatient temper of Michelangelo. Signorelli's character, from all we know of it, seems to have been most upright and generous. "Such was the goodness of his nature, that he never lent himself to things that were not just and righteous," says Vasari, [25] and that he should have been guilty of so petty a crime towards a friend, is not for a moment to be believed. Moreover, his will, re-made in the following year, proves him to have been in prosperous circumstances, while the fact that he continued to hold his appointments, and to receive fresh and even more honourable ones, testifies to the respect in which he was held by his fellow-citizens. In pleasant contrast with Michelangelo's accusation are the glimpses we have of his stately old age, through Vasari. "And at last," he writes, "having completed works for nearly [Pg 14] all the princes of Italy, and being now old, he returned to Cortona, where, in his last years, he worked more for pleasure than any other reason, as one who, accustomed to labour, knew not how to be idle." [26] Of these later paintings the "Deposition" of Umbertide proves that the old man of seventy-five had lost little of his power. It is one of his most beautiful and tender renderings of a scene he has so often painted. The "Madonna," now in the Arezzo Gallery, painted three years later (1519), shows, perhaps, a slight falling off in technical power, while retaining to the full his characteristic grandeur of conception. It was this picture which, Vasari tells us, was borne on the shoulders of the brothers, for whose order it was painted, from Cortona to Arezzo, and Luca, old as he was, insisted on accompanying them, partly to place it in position, as was customary, and partly to revisit his friends and relations. The biographer gives a characteristic incident in connection with this visit, told so charmingly, that I can do no better than transcribe it:—

"And he, being lodged in the house of the Vasari, where I was a little child of eight years, I remember how that good old man, who was always gracious and courteous, having learnt from the master who first taught me my letters, that I cared for nothing else at school but drawing pictures; I remember, I say, he turned to Antonio, my father, and said to him: 'Antonio, since Giorgio takes after his family, let him by all means be taught how to draw, because, even if he cares for literature, to know how to draw cannot but [Pg 15] be a source of honour and enjoyment, if not of utility, to him, as to every honourable man.' Then he turned to me, who stood up straight before him, and said, 'Learn, little kinsman.'" And Vasari adds, how, hearing that he suffered much from bleeding at the nose, which sometimes left him half dead, Signorelli hung a jasper charm about his neck, "with infinite tenderness. Which memory of Luca," he concludes, "will remain eternally fixed in my soul." [27] —One of those delightful human touches of which the writings of Vasari are so full.

This visit to Arezzo took place only four years before his death. He must have died in 1523, at the age of eighty-two, but there is no special record of the event, the date being gathered only from a document, which tells of the election on the 8th of December of another Inspector of Santa Margherita, to fill the place of the dead painter. [28] On the 13th of October of the same year, he had made his last will, leaving, with many minor bequests, the bulk of his property to his son, Pier Tommaso, and his grandson, Giulio, and expressing his desire to be buried in the tomb of his family in the Church of S. Francesco. [29] In his first edition, Vasari tells us that, after his death, his memory was honoured by many epitaphs, among which he quotes the following:—
"Pianga Cortona omai, vestasi oscura,
Che estinti son' del Signorello i lumi;[Pg 16]
Et tu, Pittura, fa de gli occhi fiumi,
Chè resti senza lui debili e scura." [30]
Apparently Signorelli retained his health and energy up to the end of his long life, for only the year before his death he had accepted fresh appointments in Cortona, and, in addition to his old offices, was filling those of Priore of the Fraternity of S. Mark, Sindaco del Capitans, and several others, religious and secular. He was, moreover, still actively painting, and in the very year of his death he completed the altarpiece for the Church at Foiano, a work as noble and majestic in conception as it is vigorous in execution, besides accepting a commission from the Priori to paint them an altar-piece for the chapel of their palace.

I can do no better than conclude this scanty history with the character of the man, as it is told us by Vasari: "Luca was a person of excellent habits, sincere and affectionate with his friends, sweet and agreeable in his converse with everyone, specially courteous to those who had need of his help, and kindly in his instructions to his pupils. He lived most splendidly, and delighted in dressing well. For the which good qualities he was always, in his own country and elsewhere, held in the highest veneration." [31]

FOOTNOTES:

[1] The "Madonna" (No. 281), and "The Flagellation" (No. 262), Brera, Milan.

[2] It was the fame of Lazzaro's son Giorgio as an imitator of antique vases that won for the family the name Vasari.

[3] Vasari, ii. 553.

[4] Vasari, ii. 554.

[5] Vasari, ii. 553. Editor's Notes.

[6] Vasari, iii. 683 and 684.

[7] Vasari, iii. 295.

[8] Muzi, "Memorie," p. 48; and Giacomo Mancini, "Istruzioni," ii. 66 and 67.

[9] For the dates of these various appointments, see the Chronological Table, p. 121.

[10] I have thought it best only to translate those titles which have a corresponding meaning in our own country.

[11] Vischer, p. 7.

[12] It is with the utmost diffidence I venture to hold a different opinion from a critic of such weight as Morelli (see "Italian Painters," i. 92), but a careful comparison has forced me to subscribe to the later judgments. Crowe & Cavalcaselle (see Cavalcaselle e Crowe, vi-ii. 453) and Vischer (Signorelli, p. 311) have both maintained that a great part of the execution reveals the hand of Bartolommeo della Gatta. One of the latest critics, Mr B. Berensen, presumes that the whole fresco is by him. I know too little of this painter's style to be able to form an opinion, feeling certain only that it is not by Signorelli.

[13] See Chronological Table, p. 122.

[14] Arch. dell opera del Duomo di Firenze. Deliberazioni dall'anno 1486 all'anno 1491. A Carte 77. The document merely mentions his name among those who were unable to attend.

[15] See Chronological Table, p. 122.

[16] See "Guida all'arcicenobio di Monte Oliveto" (Siena, 1844), p. 20.

[17] Proved by a document in the Orvieto Archives, containing a list of materials handed over by the Treasurer of the Works to Polidoro. See Vischer, p. 102.

[18] Now in the Opera del Duomo, Orvieto. The portrait of Signorelli in the frontispiece is the half of this painting.

[19] The letter is transcribed in Vischer, p. 356.

[20] Vasari, iii. 691.

[21] In the reprint of Cesariano's "Comments on Vitruvius," by G. B. Caporali. (Perugia, 1536). The passage is quoted in Vermiglioli's "Memorie di Pintorricchio" (1837), pp. 5 and 6.

[22] Vasari, iv. 329.

[23] The biographers of Signorelli, following the lead of Vasari, have dwelt much on his friendship with contemporary princes—the Baglioni, Vitelli, etc.; till we have grown to think of him rather as a silk-clad courtier than a hard-working burgher and painter. It may well be that, like Leonardo, he combined work with luxury, but the evidence is of too slight a nature to allow us to consider that side of his life, if it really existed. Of his friendship with Lorenzo dei Medici, however, there is more proof, since he painted for him, and was evidently influenced by his classic tastes, as several of his pictures show.

[24] The letter is transcribed in Vischer, p. 359.

[25] Vasari, iii. 683.

[26] Vasari, iii. 692.

[27] Vasari, iii. 693.

[28] Mancini, "Notizie," 94.

[29] Arch. Gen. di Contratti di Firenze. Rogiti di Ser Baldelli. Filza dal 1507 al 1524.

[30]
"Let Cortona weep henceforth, and clothe herself in black,
For the light of Signorello is extinguished;
And thou, Painting, make rivers of thine eyes
For without him thou remainest weak and obscure."

[31] Vasari, iii. 695.
[Pg 17]

CHAPTER II

DEVELOPMENT AND CHARACTERISTICS OF HIS GENIUS

The foregoing chapter contains only a bare record of certain facts in the life of Luca Signorelli. Fortunately time has spared many of his paintings, and in the study of these we get a fuller insight into his nature and his aims. A man's work is, after all, the most satisfactory and reliable document for those who take the pains to decipher it—the autobiography which every man of genius bequeaths to posterity.

We have seen how by good fortune he was placed as a child to study painting under Pier dei Franceschi, who was of all men most able to bring out in his pupils the finer instincts and nobler qualities of their genius. By his guidance and example, no doubt, Signorelli cultivated his natural breadth of conception and of treatment, which give grandeur and impressive solemnity to all his works, besides acquiring the technical excellences of good drawing, solid modelling, and the broad massing of the shadows, which are so characteristic of Piero's own painting. The spirit of master and pupil was fundamentally alike, the chief points of dissimilarity in their work arising from minor divergences of temperament. Both were men of robust mind, with a message of resolute purpose to deliver. Both chose to express themselves through [Pg 18] the medium of the human form in its most vigorous aspects, and were, therefore, pre-occupied with mastering its structure. But while Piero, with a serene nature, chose to represent unemotional figures like the sculptures of the ancient Egyptians, the restless and impetuous spirit of Signorelli preferred scenes of violent action, and energetic movement.

It was, perhaps, the entire affinity of their temperament, as well as his passion for anatomical study, which led him to choose his second master in a man whose taste for realism, and interest in the action of muscle and movement of limb was as keen as his own. On Antonio Pollaiuolo, even more than on Pier dei Franceschi, had fallen the mantle of Paolo Uccello's investigating spirit. As the latter gave all his attention to applying the laws of perspective to landscape and figures, so the efforts of Pollaiuolo were concentrated on giving freedom to the limbs. Great anatomist though he was, Piero was not so ardent a lover of the Nude for its own sake as the Florentine, and the problems of movement have little interest for him, whereas in the most characteristic work of Pollaiuolo it is evident that the scenes are chosen to display the muscles in tense prominence, and the limbs in violent action or unusual posture. [32] With precisely the same interests in the human structure and its movements, it is no wonder that Signorelli caught so much of his style and mannerisms. The influence of Antonio Pollaiuolo was stronger than [Pg 19] any other in the development of his actual work, and is visible in all his paintings up to the last in greater or less degree, but only less important is that of Donatello, to whom Antonio himself owed so much. Forty years before the birth of Signorelli, Donatello had been able to carve the human form with absolute perfection of anatomy, and not only that, but to endow it with freedom of limb and overflowing life. It is easy to suppose the impression his statues must have made on the youth, whose spirit was so much akin to his own in exuberant energy, and who had the same uncompromising love of realism. The two artists had much in common in their confident self-reliance, and almost arrogant buoyancy of nature, which was the true Renaissance expression, and the outward sign of its immense strength. Signorelli caught and revived the very essence of Donatello's spirit—the love of bodily life in its most hopeful and vigorous manifestations. It is significant that the swaggering posture which became such a special feature of his painting, should have originated with Donatello. Donatello was, before all things, a realist, and it was probably the habitual attitude of the cavalry soldier of the day, accustomed to straddle over the broad back of his war-horse, but there is little doubt that it was adopted by Signorelli from the "S. George" of Or San Michele, and perhaps half-unconsciously signified to him—what that statue so well embodies—the confident spirit of youth and strength. In his portrait of Pippo Spana, now in S. Apollonia, Florence, Andrea di Castagno also imitated and emphasised it, as also did Botticelli in his carved background of the [Pg 20] "Calumny," and Perugino in many of his paintings. But Botticelli's painted statue and Perugino's "S. Michael" and "Warriors" of the Cambio seem to spread their legs because they are too puny to bear the weight of the body in any other manner, while with Signorelli, the attitude became the keynote of his resolute indomitable nature, and so much a part of his work, that one is apt to forget it did not originate with him.

Although the character and aims of the two men are so entirely different, yet to Perugino, Signorelli owed much in his methods of producing the feeling of free space, and the life and movement of the atmosphere. Perugino's greatest gift to Art was this power of rendering the magic of the sun-warmed air and the sense of illimitable distance. He gave to his landscapes space and depth, the gentle stir of wind, and the golden shimmer of sunshine. Signorelli also learnt this power of presenting the life of hill and tree and sky, and some of his effects of distance have the space and grandeur almost of Nature herself. He also, like Perugino, could detach his figures from the background, and send the line of hills receding back to the horizon. Signorelli owes to him, besides, certain superficial characteristics, such as the fluttering scarfs and ribbon-like draperies, and the upturned face with ecstatic eyes which belongs to the Umbrian painter as much as the drooping head belongs to Botticelli.

From these four great artists Signorelli learnt what each had best to give, and assimilated and made it his own, with unerring instinct for its virtue in aiding his own specific qualities. Not that he was in any [Pg 21] sense an eclectic, but he had the unconscious tendency of the healthy soul to seize upon the food that best ministers to its nourishment. Thus the fine genius and inspiration of Pier dei Franceschi and the grace of Perugino saved him from becoming too rigorously realistic under the influence of the scientific Florentines, Donatello and Pollaiuolo, working upon his own uncompromising nature.

The most important writers on Signorelli—Crowe and Cavalcaselle, [33] Rumohr, [34] and, above all, Vischer, [35] mention several other masters, who, they claim, exercised an influence upon his work, and it is obvious that to the Sienese school generally he was indebted for many decorative methods, particularly in the use of gold and gilded gesso. There are also in some of his paintings reminiscences of Verrocchio and Fiorenzo di Lorenzo; but an impression of sufficient depth to be considered, must touch the spirit, and here there appears to me to be little besides superficial resemblances. It must be remembered, moreover, in the case of Verrocchio, how much he himself owed to Donatello, while with respect to the asserted influence of Pintorricchio, it is more probable that what likeness there is in their style should testify to the impression of the stronger upon the weaker nature. With Andrea di Castagno his work, both in outward form and in spirit, has something in common; and no doubt Signorelli was impressed by paintings which themselves show so much the influence of Donatello. [Pg 22]

As we have seen, Luca's chief interest, like that of Pollaiuolo, lay in the effort to render movement of limb with facility, and therefore his attention was concentrated on the muscles and their action. We do not know how long he studied anatomy from the dead and living model in the Florentine workshop, nor have we any example of his gradual development, for when he first appears before us in his earliest remaining work, "The Flagellation," of the Brera, he is already the master who has conquered all the difficulties of muscular movement, and surpassed even Antonio Pollaiuolo in freedom of gesture and correct anatomy.

It is not till later, however, that the most important advance he made on previous painting first begins to show itself—the power, namely, of rendering combined action, of working the limbs of a crowd into a single movement. This is Signorelli's special achievement, on the merits of which he takes rank with the most important masters of the Quattrocento as a pioneer and teacher. Great as was Pollaiuolo's command over gesture and action, it was limited to the combination of two figures only, [36] while with Signorelli the action of the single figure is held subordinate to that of the multitude. He gives the stately march of an army, as in the Umbertide predella and the Monte Oliveto fresco; the writhings of innumerable figures, like heaps of coiled serpents, as in the "Damnation" [Pg 23] of Orvieto; the rush of a violent mob stirred by a common impulse, as in the Florence and Cortona "Betrayals." This command over united movement was new in painting, though, like all other difficulties, it had been already mastered by Donatello, as we see in his romping children of the Prato pulpit, and the Florence Cantoria, to name only two examples. Botticelli, who, with so different a nature, had yet, in common with the robust Signorelli, this passion for swift movement, achieved later, it is true, almost as great triumphs [37] ; but to Luca belongs the merit of having endowed painting with the same freedom of combined movement which Donatello had given to sculpture.

Unlike Botticelli, he is consistently a lover of energy all through his life, and as the source of energy, of strength, and vigorous health. His grand conception of the body is one of the chief characteristics of his work. Strong and stately, it is a fit receptacle for the spirit of resolution and self-confidence with which he animates it. His Virgins are like goddesses, and seem to typify for him the strength of womanhood. Nowhere do we see nobler beauty than in his angels and archangels. In these "divine birds" [38] he seems to have recognised the ideal of all he strove for, and their wings are symbols to him of swift movement and superhuman strength. It was always strength that attracted him, and strength conscious of its own force, [Pg 24] finding its expression in exuberant animation. Thus he loves to paint the swaggering soldiers, whose attitudes express their audacious self-reliance. He gives the luxuriant life of Nature as no one else gave it, and his trees and plants are as robust and unyielding as his firmly-planted figures. His angels' wings are not merely decorative, but have real power of muscle under the plumes to lift the body and bear it aloft without fatigue.

He was a lover of beauty, but it was not for beauty he strove, or we should not so often find bits of realistic ugliness to risk the harmony of his noblest paintings. Grace and charm seemed to come to him unsought, as natural adjuncts of a vigorous and healthy nature; but his deliberate choice of types of face and form, were those which, by their strength, promised satisfaction to his love of energetic action. From the first this tendency is noticeable, for example, in the above-mentioned "Flagellation," and the Loreto "Conversion of Saul," and goes on increasing until it reaches a climax in the frescoes of Orvieto.

Once one has grasped the main motive of Signorelli's work, his preoccupation with movement, and consequently with the muscles, his frequent defects and inequalities in other respects become, as faults of inattention, less incomprehensible. For example, his values of distance are often faulty, and give the unpleasant sensation that one figure is standing on the top of another, [39] a defect of carelessness, for no one is a better master of aerial perspective when he chooses. [Pg 25] Again, his hands and feet are often incorrectly drawn and badly modelled, but it is only when they are not essential to the action; for although the drawing of hands and feet is always perhaps his weakest point, yet even in his early painting of the "Flagellation" he has already mastered some of their greatest difficulties of foreshortening. The recognition of the intention in a man's work enables one to dispense with much adverse criticism in detail. It would be wearisome to reiterate the faults of drawing in each picture when we come to deal with them separately, and it is better to recognise in the outset that, in pursuit of a certain definite end, Signorelli is careless of what seems to him unessential at the moment.

Thus in dealing with him as a colourist [40] we have to bear in mind that it was by line and modelling chiefly that his effects of movement were obtained. To be over-critical of the shortcomings of his colour, therefore, would be as foolish as to miss the charm of Bonifazio's splendid harmonies in abuse of some defect of drawing. Sometimes, in fact, Signorelli gains his end by the very crudeness and heaviness for which he is generally condemned, the sharp contrasts giving a rugged strength to his painting, and the copper colour of the flesh adding robustness to the figures.

It would, however, be most unjust to speak as if his colour were always, or even usually, crude and harsh. On the contrary, in landscape it is invariably beautiful; and he uses certain golden and moss-greens in foliage and grass, and a limpid greenish-blue in [Pg 26] water, which are most harmonious. Sometimes it is gorgeous, and in nearly all his early paintings there is a beauty of red and soft green, and a warmth of golden glow of great depth and tenderness. He had, perhaps, a tendency to the use of too heavy colour, especially in the flesh; and he himself seems aware of it, for, in middle life, for a brief time, he changed his tone to an almost silvery lightness, with very pale flesh-tints, as in the Uffizi "Holy Family," No. 1291, and again, after working at Orvieto, in the "Dead Christ supported by Angels," of S. Niccolò, Cortona, whose general colour is almost like honey; but he relapses always into his characteristic dark tones, especially in the works of his old age, which are for the most part heavy and rather harsh, with flesh-tints of the reddish-brown of terra-cotta.

It is, as I have said, by form rather than colour that Signorelli obtains his best effects. He is a superb linealist, as the often-quoted "Flagellation" shows, and one is inclined to wish he had oftener used outline, as here, in the manner of Pier dei Franceschi. His line is firm and clear, simple and structural, of unerring sweep and accuracy, as we see in his numerous *predella* paintings; but even more remarkable is the wonderful plastic quality of his modelling. By this he makes us realise better than any one before him the tenseness of sinew, the resistance of hard muscle, and the supple elasticity of flesh, giving a solidity and weight to his forms that make them impressive as grand sculptures.

As an illustrator Signorelli is most unequal; brilliant and dramatic when the subject appealed to his taste, [Pg 27] as in the Orvieto frescoes, often weak, as in his treatment of sacred themes. He was essentially a religious painter, but in the widest meaning of the word, and he does not seem to have felt the dignity and significance of many of the scenes in the life of Christ. When he has to paint Him bound to the pillar or nailed to the Cross, submissive to scourging and insult, his interest seems to wander from what should be the central figure, and fixes itself on some two or three of the minor actors, to whom he gives the importance he should have concentrated on the Christ. The painter *con amore* of arrogant strength, he seems to have little in common with meekness and humility that bows the head to scourging and martyrdom. Thus in nearly all his "Crucifixions" the central figure is ignoble in type and expression, and in the "Flagellations" of the Brera and of Morra, is entirely without dignity, even ignominious. This is curious when we consider that even more than of arrogant strength Signorelli was the painter of stately and noble beauty.

Again it seems as if he cared only to represent figures of powerful maturity, for there is a complete lack of sympathy in his painting of children. With one or two exceptions, his child Christs are half-animal little beings, more like tiny satyrs than human children, although not without a certain pathos in their very ugliness. In a picture of as great beauty and tender feeling as the "Holy Family," of the Rospigliosi Collection, for example, the child is more animal than human. Unlike Donatello, who delights in childhood, and sees in it the bubbling source of future strength, [Pg 28] Signorelli gives his babies the overweighted, unelastic sadness of old age. In composing his Holy Families, therefore, his attention is centred on the Virgin, the strong woman he loved to paint, but the child he seems to feel as an accessory to be executed because the Church has ordered it, and so he puts it in without thought of all it meant and typified.

But although he sometimes falls short as an interpreter of the Church's intention, the impressive grandeur of his work is in itself intensely religious, and he makes us feel most solemnly the dignity of Nature, and especially of the human form. Once he was stirred into something of the Pagan spirit, probably under the influence of the court of Lorenzo, and he touched the real note of Pantheism in the "Pan," of the Berlin Gallery, and the noble figures in the background of the Uffizi and Munich "Madonnas." In these the spiritual mood dominates and is sustained throughout, and there is no sign of the scientific absorption which sometimes in his treatment of the nude makes us too aware of the student and the realist. One is at times conscious that, painting straight from the life, Signorelli's interest lay chiefly in a faithful reproduction of the body before him. His dead Christs for example, were obviously copied exactly as the corpses lay or hung in his studio. The S. Onofrio of the Perugia altarpiece, stood just so, a half-starved street-beggar, with baggy skin over rheumatic joints. The angel in the same picture, chosen perhaps for its grace of face, must be reproduced exactly as the child sat, with weak legs and ungainly body. Each figure is a truthful study from life, and it was that which interested the painter, [Pg 29] and not that he was representing saints and angels whose noble beauty was supposed to elevate the mind to a state of worship.

Yet with all his realistic treatment, he was intensely alive to the graces of decoration, both in general lines and in detail. In the frescoes of Loreto, and more particularly of Orvieto, the mere scheme of decoration is superb, and adds beauty and distinction to every subtle line of the architecture. He pays attention, also, to the minor details of decorative effect, and takes pains with the ornaments and embroideries; while his use of gold, and embossing with gesso, add much to the æsthetic charm of his work, and proves that he could, when necessary, subordinate his love of realism to his sense of beauty.

Before summing up the chief qualities of Signorelli's work, I must not omit one characteristic which points to the strength of his personality—the way he repeats his own types (and not types only, but precisely the same forms) time after time, and often after the lapse of many years. The child Christs he paints over and over again, the same figure, sometimes exactly in the same attitude, as in the "Madonnas," of the Florence Academy and of the Brera. The seated burly Bishop of the Loreto vaulting (one of his earliest works) occurs again in the Volterra "Madonna," and again (painted many years later) in the "Madonna," of the Florence Academy. Line for line he reproduces the figure of Echo, out of the early "Pan," into the fresco of "The Crowning of the Elect," at Orvieto. In one or two cases he boldly repeats the same figure in the same picture, feature for feature, as in the Virgin and [Pg 30] S. John of the Rospigliosi "Holy Family," limb for limb as in the flying soldiers of the Loreto "Conversion of Saul."

He was also most faithful to his own type of limb or feature, especially those in which Morelli has taught us always to look for similarity. The fleshy ear, with its slightly pointed top, is nearly invariable, as also is the broad hand with its little outlined nails and thick wrists.

In glancing rapidly over the whole of Signorelli's work, consistency to an absorbing interest is the note struck again and again. He has set himself from the first a task—the mastery of the human structure and its movements; and with the resolution and perseverance of a strong nature, he never swerves from his purpose. This is the conscious aim and intention of the artist. What he was able to give to the world, of nobility and dignity—a wider and healthier conception of Nature and her power and beauty—was the Message of his Genius, of which he was himself unconscious, but which spoke all the more forcibly for the learning acquired by hard application and earnest effort. In a detailed study of his painting, it may be that the student of anatomy and the realist often assert themselves, but as grand figure after grand figure has passed before the mind, the general impression is solemn and ennobling. "To no other contemporary painter," says Morelli, "was it given to endow the human frame with the like degree of passion, vehemence and strength." [41] To this we may add that no other painter has ever conceived Humanity [Pg 31] with the same stately grandeur and in the same broad spirit. The confident strength of youth, the stern austerity of middle life, the resolute solemnity of old age—these are his themes. Signorelli is, before all, the painter of the dignity of human life.

FOOTNOTES:

[32] It is sufficient to cite the double picture of "Hercules," of the Uffizi, the "S. Sebastian," of the National Gallery, and the engraving called "The Battle of the Nudes."

[33] Cavalcaselle e Crowe, viii. 424, etc.

[34] Ital. Forsch. ii. 333.

[35] Vischer, 77, etc. Vischer considers the likeness to Fiorenzo due to their mutual relation to Verrocchio.

[36] Even the splendid decorative engraving called "The Battle of the Nudes," is only a series of duels. A comparison of these figures with the two nude executioners in the Brera "Flagellation" will justify the assertion of Signorelli's superiority as a master of anatomy and movement.

[37] Specially in "The Death of Virginia," of the Morelli Collection, Bergamo, and the sketched figures in the repainted "Adoration of the Magi," lately exposed in the Uffizi.

[38] "Purgatorio," ii. 38.

[39] For example, in the "Madonna," of the Mancini Collection, and "The Crowning of the Elect," at Orvieto.

[40] Signorelli's pictures, when not frescoed, are invariably painted with oil.

[41] "Italian Painters," i. 92. [Pg 32]

CHAPTER III

EARLIEST WORKS

One of the most remarkable things in the history of Signorelli's work, considering what a number of his paintings remain, is that only two of them can be placed with any degree of certainty as having been executed before his fortieth year. These two are the "Madonna" (No. 281), and "The Flagellation" (No. 262), in the Brera Gallery, Milan. This last, however—"The Flagellation"—indicates in what manner much of his earlier time had been employed, for although betraying in parts a certain youthful immaturity, yet the skilful drawing and thorough comprehension of anatomy shown in the nudes, especially in the backs of the two executioners, reveals already the practised hand of a master of his craft.

[Brera, Milan
THE FLAGELLATION
The best studies of the nude remaining to us by earlier painters, are the figures in "The Death of Adam," by Pier dei Franceschi, in his frescoes at Arezzo, the "Hercules overcoming Antæus," and "The Battle of the Nudes," by Antonio Pollaiuolo, in the Uffizi Gallery. It is sufficient to compare with these the freer rendering of gesture, and the

greater accuracy of the anatomy in Signorelli's executioners, to see what an advance he had already made upon any previous painting. (I limit, of course, this assertion to painting [Pg 33] only, for in sculpture Donatello had years before given free gesture and perfect anatomy to his statues.) It would be impossible to overrate the excellence and beauty of drawing in the splendid swing of the bodies, the flexibility of the limbs, the sinewy elasticity of the leg muscles, and above all, the subtle suggestion of muscular movement under the loose skin of the backs. There is here, even more than in his later painting, an appreciation of the relative values of the muscles, and a consequent breadth of modelling, which he lost somewhat, by over-accentuation, in his subsequent treatment of the nude. The inequalities of the picture betray wherein lay the painter's chief interest, for to this skilful mastery of the difficulties of anatomy are opposed the rather childish conception of the Pilate and the stiff action of all the clothed figures. His apprenticeship to Pier dei Franceschi is here sufficiently proved, not so much by any likeness of colour or of composition to "The Flagellations," of that master, in Urbino and Borgo San Sepolero, as in the firm, clear outlining of the nude figures, their solid modelling, and in the broad massing of the shadows.

Even more apparent is the influence of Antonio Pollaiuolo, in the great realism with which the subject is treated, and in such superficial resemblances as the type of head of the executioner who binds the hands of Christ, and the characteristic striped loin-cloths.

The Christ is one of Signorelli's most ignoble presentations of the Saviour, and yet it seems as though he had tried to give graces which should harmonise with a certain conception of the character—the hair, for example, is the beautiful rippling hair of a woman, the [Pg 34] bent head and downcast eyes represent the gentleness of resignation, and the attitude of the legs is intended to be graceful. But the effort to curb his own natural instinct for pride and strength makes him strike a false note, and his attempt to give the beauty of meekness has resulted only in producing a mask of hypocritical inertia.

The picture was painted for the Church of Santa Maria del Mercato in Fabriano, and this, as well as the fact of its being precisely the same size, and with the same curved top, seems to argue that it formed originally one picture with the Madonna, No. 281 of the same gallery, whose *provenance* is also from that church. Here the Virgin sits, [42] clad in a gold garment and blue green-lined mantle, with the Child on her knee, and floating round her dark-green cherubs' heads. She is the powerful type of woman, from which in his Virgins Signorelli never departed, but in this case with a rather cow-like expression, which gave place later to a tender or noble dignity. The face of the Child has lost its original character through re-painting, but the cherubs' heads surrounding the throne, have the over-weighted, half-animal expression of which I have already spoken as characteristic of his children.

Next in order, as far as can be judged by the internal evidence of the painting, come the frescoes in the sacristy of the church of the Santa Casa at Loreto. They were finished some time before 1484, and bear very marked traces of Florentine impressions. Of these [Pg 35] Vasari writes: "In Santa Maria di Loreto, he painted in the sacristy in fresco, the four Evangelists, the four Doctors, and other Saints, which are very beautiful; and for this work he was liberally rewarded by Pope Sixtus." [43] This is a mistake, for the patron of the church was Cardinal Girolamo Basso della Rovere, and the presence of his coat-of-arms in the centre of the cupola is evidence that the work was executed at his expense.

In each of the eight compartments of this roof is painted a standing angel, playing or tuning musical instruments—most graceful and beautiful figures. Below are seated the four Evangelists and four Fathers of the Church, against a gold background, who seem, in their impressive grandeur to be prototypes of the prophets and sybils of Michelangelo's Sistine frescoes. I do not agree with Vischer in seeing the hand of Bartolommeo della Gatta in the angels. They show much of the influence of Pollaiuolo, and seem to me to be Signorelli's unassisted work. The face and gesture of one of them especially—the angel in the flowered robe playing a lute—is almost a duplicate of the child on the *gradino* of the throne in the Perugia altar-piece. The bishop in the compartment next this angel is repeated in the Volterra "Madonna and Saints," and in that of the Florence Academy.

[*Santa Casa, Loreto*
APOSTLES

In the divisions of the walls under the roof are painted the twelve Apostles, grand and stately figures, standing two in each compartment, divided by imitation pilasters, and forming a magnificent frieze round the walls. The draperies are exceedingly broadly painted [Pg 36] and this breadth of treatment and the boldness of the design gives importance to the figures. There being seven compartments to be filled, in two of them Signorelli has introduced the figure of Christ, treated this time with dignity, perhaps because here He is represented as the Master, and not the "Man of Sorrows." In one He reproves S. Peter (?), who turns away with conscience-stricken humility very nobly rendered; in the other He shows the marks of the Passion to the incredulous Thomas. These two are perhaps the finest of the series, and are, besides, dramatic in gesture and expression. The composition of the last is, with evident intention, borrowed from Verrocchio's group on the walls of Or San Michele, Florence, but the likeness ends with the general lines of composition. Vischer makes a strong point of this, as a proof of Verrocchio's influence on Signorelli, [44] but to me it seems that feeling, types of face, and especially the broad and simple treatment of the draperies are entirely different.

[*Santa Casa, Loreto*]
THE INCREDULITY OF S. THOMAS

The most important of these frescoes, however, as best illustrating Signorelli's own peculiar tendencies, is "The Conversion of Saul," in the compartment over the door. He has realised the scene with emotion, and rendered it with a most convincing dramatic power, giving the suddenness of the fall of the principal figure, and the excitement and panic-stricken terror of the soldiers, with wonderful truth and animation. It is interesting to note the almost exact repetition of the same figure in the two soldiers who hurry away to the left, but it is not at all mechanical, and in no way [Pg 37] detracts from the excellence of the composition. Very Pollaiuolesque is the figure with raised shield in the foreground to the right, and one feels the influence of Perugino in the spacious empty distance of the background, from which the figures are so well detached.

[*Santa Casa, Loreto*]
THE CONVERSION OF SAUL

As decoration these frescoes are exceedingly fine, the grand row of figures, besides the stately strength of each separate group, being most impressive in general effect. They have been much damaged. For many years used as a sacristy, the greasy smoke of the incense had so blackened the walls that the frescoes were nearly invisible. The skilful cleaning of Signor Guiseppe Missaghi, at the instigation of Signor Cavalcaselle, has restored to them much of their original beauty, although the colour still remains somewhat obscured.

On the roof of the nave, in the church itself, are painted a series of frescoes in *grisaille*, twenty-six Prophets and Fathers of the Church, somewhat over life size, seated one in each medallion. They are solemn and impressive figures like those in the sacristy, and painted on the same broad lines, and remind one strongly of the two medallions, also in *grisaille*, in the "Madonna," of the Uffizi Corridor. All of them have severely suffered from repainting.

"The Adoration of the Magi," formerly in the Campana Gallery, Rome, now No. 389 of the Louvre, seems to have been painted in 1482. Crowe and Cavalcaselle [45] rightly consider its execution to be the work of assistants, by reason of the rawness of colour and general coarseness of the painting; yet in composition, and in many of [Pg 38] the figures, there is so much of the master's impressive dignity, that I feel compelled to regard the drawing, in parts at least, as his own. The stately Madonna, and the noble figure of the King on her right, whose draperies have the same sweeping breadth as those in the National Gallery, "Circumcision," as well as the solid, well-seated figures of the mounted attendants, seem to be Signorelli's own composing. The Child is also characteristic, and resembles that in the *Tondo* of the Pitti Gallery. The badly-drawn horses, again, seem his, for it will be noticed all through his work that he has never cared to thoroughly master their form, and paints them always with curious mannerisms of too closely-placed nostrils, and human eyebrows, which show how little attention he had given to their anatomy.

The first dated picture remaining is the altar-piece of the Perugia Cathedral, painted in 1484, of which Vasari writes: "Also in Perugia he painted many works; and among others in the Cathedral, for Messer Jacopo Vannucci of Cortona, Bishop of the city, a picture in which is Our Lady, Sant Onofrio, Sant Ercolano, S. John Baptist, S. Stephen, [46] and an angel, most beautiful, who tunes a lute." [47] The inscription with the date (given in the catalogue) are unfortunately hidden by the frame. This is one of Signorelli's finest altar-pieces, the colour being especially rich and harmonious, and it shows, even more than the Loreto frescoes, the strength of Florentine influences. For example, very close to Pollaiuolo is the figure of the angel tuning the lute, [Pg 39] with its striped scarf, and so also is the powerful head of S. Ercolano. The S. Stephen is almost a reproduction of the bust of S. Lorenzo by Donatello in the sacristy of the church of that saint in Florence, the aged S. Onofrio again recalls his wooden statue of S. Jerome in Faenza, and finally the motive of the cut flowers in glasses is borrowed from the triptych of Hugo van der Goes in the Gallery of Santa Maria Nuova, Florence. The ornamental accessories are singularly fine and careful in finish, and it would seem as though Signorelli had been inspired in this, not only by the great tryptych, but also by the followers of the Paduan Squarcione. In the last chapter I have pointed out the extreme realism with which the figures are treated, but this does not spoil the impressive grandeur of the painting, gained by the broad style and the stately simplicity of the composition. The Virgin sits firmly, with the mantle resting in heavy folds across her knees; the S. Stephen is overflowing with the vigorous life of youth; the splendidly-draped bishop is a powerful and majestic figure; and there is real tenderness and grace in the face of the angel, notwithstanding the want of symmetry in the body and legs. The painting has suffered from restoration, but on the whole is fairly well preserved, and may be seen to advantage in the quiet of this well-lighted winter-chapel.

[*Cathedral, Perugia*
MADONNA AND SAINTS

Crowe and Cavalcaselle place "The Circumcision," of the National Gallery, formerly in Volterra, as about the same date as the foregoing; [48] Vischer, presuming that it was painted at the same time with the dated pictures of 1491 still remaining in Volterra, groups it with them; [Pg 40] but the similarity of colour and treatment lead me to accept the former theory. The distance from Cortona to Volterra is not very great, and the fact that he was painting there in 1491 does not preclude the possibility of his having painted there six or seven years before, even if it was executed on the spot, which was not by any means always the case. At all events the picture has much in common with the Perugia altar-piece, both in warmth of colour, simplicity of composition and splendid breadth of execution. The painting of this "Circumcision" is bold and resolute, the draperies sweep in broad folds round the figures. The attitude of the standing woman to the right is grand, and the earnest concentration of the faces on the ceremony, and the absence of any connecting link between them and us, give dramatic reality to the scene. Vasari writes of it: "At Volterra he painted in fresco"—(a mistake—it is his usual oil medium)—"in the church of S. Francesco, above the altar of the brotherhood, the Circumcision of our Lord, which is considered marvellously beautiful; although the Child, having suffered from the damp, was repainted by Sodoma much less beautiful than it was before." [49] This unfortunate repainting, which has also evidently included part of the Virgin's face, was more probably due to the monks' dislike of Signorelli's type of child than to any damage by weather, for it would be strange that a picture, otherwise so well preserved, should be injured by damp nowhere but in the part most protected by reason of its central position. To support this theory, under the painting by Sodoma may be clearly seen (in the painting [Pg 41] —not in the photograph) the original legs of the Child of Signorelli, in a totally different position, showing that Sodoma had made no attempt to keep to the drawing. The monks, no doubt, preferred the more commonplace infant of Sodoma, but we, while acknowledging that the children of Signorelli are far from what they should be, may regret the loss, as did Vasari, who adds this comment: "It would be better to retain the work of excellent men, even though half spoiled, than to have it repainted by one who knows less."

[*National Gallery, London*
THE CIRCUMCISION

A very important group of paintings apparently of about this date, bear the impress of the classic tastes of the Court of Lorenzo dei Medici, for whom they seem to have been painted. It comprises the great picture of "Pan," in the Berlin Gallery, the "Madonna," of the Uffizi Corridor, and the Munich *Tondo*. I have been tempted to give them a much earlier place, in the gap before the Perugia altar-piece, because they show so much of the idealism and idyllic spirit, which seem properly to belong to youth, but a careful comparison of them with that picture and the Loreto frescoes, reveals a greater maturity of technique which makes so early a placing not very probable. In all these three paintings there is an appreciation of beauty for its own sake, and a true touch of the Pantheistic spirit, combined with a melancholy grandeur, which is most impressive.

The finest of the three, the great canvas of "Pan," now in the Berlin Gallery, is the picture of which Vasari wrote: "He painted for Lorenzo dei Medici, on canvas, some nude gods, which were much praised . and presented to the said Lorenzo." [50] Sometimes [Pg 42] called the "School of Pan," it is more poetically described in the German catalogue "Pan, as God of Natural Life, and Master of Music, with his Attendants." It is full of poetry, and of idyllic charm with all its stately solemnity. The sad beauty of the god as he listens to the music of the pipes, the golden sunlight on the moss-green grass, the quiet peace of the scene, have an entrancing effect, and we are transported in spirit to the same "melodious plot of beechen green and shadows numberless" where Pan holds his court.

[*Gallery, Berlin*
PAN

The bronze-coloured body of the god is magnificently modelled, with a solidity unequalled even in the Orvieto frescoes. The style of Pollaiuolo is noticeable, in the attitude of the youth lying at his feet, particularly in the treatment of the legs. The figure of Echo is repeated later in "The Crowning of the Elect," in Orvieto, though there it has lost much of the idyllic charm of this wood-nymph. The grouping of the figures is perhaps less happy than usual, but this time the bad values of distance are no doubt due to the rough treatment the painting has undergone. It has indeed had an eventful history. About thirty years ago it was found by the late Signor Tricca, a noted restorer of pictures, in the attics of the Palazzo Corsi, Florence. He hesitated at first to recognise it certainly as the work of Signorelli, for all the figures were covered from head to foot with draperies of obviously eighteenth-century painting. On trial, however, he found that these were easily removed, and as the nude figures were revealed, he at once identified it as the picture of the nude gods, mentioned by Vasari. [Pg 43] It seems that it had passed into the possession of the Rinuccini family as part of the dowry of one of the Medici, and on the marriage of one of the ladies of the Rinuccini with a Marchese Corsi again formed part of the bride's portion. Soon after its discovery and restoration the Marchese Corsi died, and his brother Cardinal Corsi inherited the property. Objecting to the picture on account of the nude figures, he desired Signor Tricca to sell it, and it was then bought by Mr H. J. Ross, who offered it to the English National Gallery. On the refusal of the authorities to purchase it, it was acquired in 1873 by Dr Bode for the Berlin Gallery, of which it is one of the greatest treasures. [51] It has naturally suffered much from the process of cleaning away the later draperies, and much of the underpainting is exposed, but enough remains of its original beauty to rank it as the best of Signorelli's easel pictures.

Undoubtedly of the same date is the "Madonna," No. 74 of the Uffizi Gallery. This picture was, also, according to Vasari, painted as a present for Lorenzo dei Medici, and was for many years in the villa of Duke Cosimo at Castello. It has the same idyllic beauty in the background as the "Pan," and is painted in the same half-pagan spirit. The Virgin, it is true, sits awkwardly, and with a rather ungainly gesture of hands and arms, there are faults of drawing in the feet, and the Child is ugly and insignificant. But these are faults easy to overlook in considering the grandeur of the landscape, the beauty of the colour, [Pg 44] and, above all, the magnificent modelling of the nude figures in the background. The Virgin gains in importance by the nobility of these athletes behind her, but it is clear that Signorelli's interest lay less in the melancholy Mother and Child, than in these superb Titans, in whom he seems to have personified the forces of Nature. How great was the influence of this picture upon Michelangelo we need only take a few steps into the Tribuna to see, in his *Tondo* of the Holy Family, No. 1139. The painting is set in a kind of frame in *grisaille*, surmounted by a head of S. John the Baptist, and two seated Prophets in medallions.

[*Uffizi, Florence*
MADONNA

Somewhat inferior in execution, but painted in exactly the same spirit, is the "Madonna," of the Munich Gallery, formerly in the Palazzo Ginori, Florence. [52] Here, as in the last, the Virgin sits, filling the foreground space, a stately figure, with fingers pressed together, as if in prayer to the Child at her feet. The background is a classic landscape, through which runs a stream of the beautiful limpid green with which Signorelli always paints water, and by its side sits another of the noble nude figures, untying his sandal. It may be intended for S. John the Baptist, as the critics say, but I do not think that either here or in the Uffizi painting, Signorelli had any intention of adhering to traditional illustration. It seems rather as though the pictures were symbolic—expressive of some comparison in his mind between Christianity, as he perhaps conceived it for the moment, melancholy [Pg 45] and dejected, and the Greek Pantheism, vigorous and strong, and radiant with the joy of life.

Another picture belonging to this beautiful group is the "Portrait of a Man," in the Berlin Gallery, formerly in the Torrigiani Collection, Florence. In the days before it was photographed it was considered to be a portrait of Signorelli himself, and, as it represents a man with grey hair, was naturally reckoned among his later works; but comparison with the two portraits at Orvieto show that there is no real resemblance of feature, while the technique and spirit of the painting claim a place for it among this early series.

Here again occur the classic figures, but this time with less of the idyllic feeling. On one side are hurrying Apollo and Daphne(?), on the other, one athlete has overthrown another, and stands menacingly over his prey, who tries with ineffectual gestures to beat him off—a very Pollaiuolesque scene of violence. The colouring, with its clear reds of the *biretta* and the robe, is very successful. With this powerful portrait closes this beautiful and interesting group of paintings, the *provenance* of all four of which, it will be observed, is from Florence.

The two *Tondos*, of the Pitti and Corsini Galleries, Florence, must have been painted at a date not far distant from those, for they have much in common in certain forms, and particularly in the rich and glowing scheme of colour.

The "Holy Family," of the Pitti Gallery, has been restored, and suffers much from thick varnish and repainting, but nothing has spoilt the harmony of [Pg 46] the colours, nor the tender beauty of the Virgin, whose features and expression are a repetition of those of Echo in the "Pan." The Saint, who writes at the dictation of the Child, is painted with earnestness, and the whole scene is treated with the utmost religious feeling.

The "Madonna and Saints," of the Corsini Gallery, has the same warm glow of colour, and was probably painted about the same time. The Virgin sits with the Child on her left knee, clad in a red robe, round the neck of which little Loves are embroidered in gold. Over it she wears a dark-green mantle shot with gold—a form of decoration very usual with Signorelli, especially about this time. She has the beautiful, pale, honey-coloured hair which occurs so often in his works, almost the same colour which was characteristic of Palma's Venetian ladies later. To the left kneels S. Jerome, gazing up at her, and on the right is S. Bernard holding a pen and book. The painting is in a good state of preservation.

[*Pitti, Florence*
MADONNA AND SAINTS

The rather insignificant type of head of S. Joseph occurs again in another "Holy Family," which belongs approximately to the same period,—that of the Rospigliosi Gallery in Rome. As far as beauty and tender grace go, this is the most successful of all his Madonnas. The daring repetition of the same features with darker colouring in the S. John behind her, I have already drawn attention to. The draperies are painted with great freedom, and a fine sweep of broad fold. They are shot, as in the Corsini *Tondo*, with gold in the high lights. Insignificant as is the Child in all these Holy Families, there is at the same [Pg 47] time something pathetic and winning in the earnest, careworn little face.

[*Rospigliosi Gallery, Rome*
HOLY FAMILY

Very different is the type Signorelli has adopted for the Christ in the Uffizi "Holy Family," No. 1291, which must be placed somewhere about this time, or a very little later. Here He is represented with a certain nobility of feature and gesture, although self-conscious and unchildlike. The Greek profile of the Virgin is almost identical with that of the above-mentioned Rospigliosi picture, while the powerful head of S. Joseph

carries us back to the figures in the "Circumcision." The Virgin sits uneasily, ill-balanced, and with badly-modelled feet, but the beauty of the face makes amends for these defects. It is a picture full of noble qualities, both of feeling and technique, and it has besides a special importance by reason of the difference of colour, so much less heavy than usual. The flesh tints are very pale, and the shadows a silvery grey, and the whole tone is much lighter than in any of the preceding pictures. The composition is specially fine, the attention being concentrated without effort on the central figure of the Child, to which the other two serve as a kind of frame.

[*Uffizi, Florence*
HOLY FAMILY

I cannot leave this series of early works, which includes so many *Tondos*, without drawing attention to the excellence of Signorelli's composition in this difficult form. The figures fill the space naturally and without any artificial bending of the heads to fit the shape; there is a sense of space, and ease of grouping, and the large sweeping lines of the draperies follow most harmoniously the curves of the panel.

With the exception of the Perugia altar-piece, none [Pg 48] of the above-mentioned paintings are dated. Inferentially we arrive at the time when the Loreto frescoes were completed, but there is little to help in grouping the rest beyond the internal evidence they afford. I have endeavoured to place them in the order they seem most naturally to take, with reference to colour, form, and the early influences to be observed in them, but the arrangement must necessarily be somewhat arbitrary.

Fortunately this difficulty grows less and less in dealing with the later works, and the most important of them are generally dated.

FOOTNOTES:

[42] I shall, as far as space permits, describe those pictures of which illustrations cannot be inserted. Where the illustration is given, it becomes unnecessary.

[43] Vasari, iii. 691.
[44] Vischer, p. 79.
[45] Cavalcaselle e Crowe, viii. 507. Note 1.
[46] I have thought it best only to translate those names that are familiar to us in English.
[47] Vasari, iii. 685.
[48] Cavalcaselle e Crowe, viii. 455.
[49] Vasari, iii. 685.
[50] Vasari, iii. 689.
[51] I am indebted for the above facts to Mr H. J. Ross of Poggio Gherardo, Florence, the original purchaser of the picture.
[52] The photograph gives so little idea of the beauty of the original that I have not reproduced it.
[Pg 49]

CHAPTER IV
MIDDLE PERIOD

We have now arrived at the paintings belonging to the year 1491, part of which Signorelli spent in Volterra, three works still remaining in that city to testify to the visit—"The Annunciation," of the Cathedral; the "Madonna and Saints," now in the Gallery, both dated; and a much-injured fresco in *grisaille*, representing S. Jerome, on the walls of the same building—the Palazzo Communale.

The "Madonna enthroned with Saints" was painted for the altar of Maffei Chapel in San Francesco, and was unfortunately removed not many years ago to the Gallery of the Palazzo Communale, suffering the greatest damage in the transit. Two large cracks run through the figures of the Child and the seated Father; large pieces of the paint have dropped away, and in the repainting the Child has lost all characteristics of Signorelli's work. In the less ruined parts, however, enough remains to testify to the original excellence of the painting, which is finely composed, and broadly and vigorously treated, especially in the draperies.

The Virgin sits enthroned between four saints, with a very Peruginesque angel on either side, and seated below, at the foot of her throne, are two Fathers of the [Pg 50] Church, in one of whom we have repeated the burly bishop with wide-spread knees and fine sweeping drapery of the Loreto cupola, and which occurs later in the Florence Academy altar-piece. The influence of Pollaiuolo can be observed in the sculptures on the *gradino* of the throne, little nude figures in violent action.

In better preservation is the "Annunciation," in the Cathedral, signed, and with the same date as the foregoing. The architecture, with its excellent perspective, again reminds us that Signorelli was the pupil of Pier dei Franceschi, the painter of the wonderful *loggia* in the "Annunciation," of Perugia. The Virgin is painted with great feeling, and in the solemn beauty of the Archangel we get the first of those splendid creatures whose sublimity Signorelli felt in the same spirit as Dante, who bent his knees and folded his hands at the sight of the "*Uccel divino*," "*trattando l'aere con l'eterne penne.*" [53]

[Cathedral, Volterra
THE ANNUNCIATION

The resemblance is so great between this painting and the "Annunciation," of the Uffizi *predella* (No. 1298) that we are justified in placing the latter somewhere about the same date. As is so often the case in *predella* pictures, especially with Signorelli's, the spontaneity and freedom of execution, and even of conception, is much greater here than in the more carefully thought-out and finished works. Small as this panel is, the rush of the great Archangel, the solemn beauty of the landscape, and the splendid attitudes of the young courtiers in the last division, make it one of the master's most important and [Pg 51] characteristic paintings. The colour in the first panel of the "Annunciation" is especially beautiful, and there is a noble simplicity in the composition, as well as a breadth and certainty of touch that give the picture great grandeur. The *predella* is divided by painted pilasters into three parts. In the first the Archangel hastens through a rocky pass to announce the message, to which the Virgin bows with awed acceptance of its solemn meaning. In the second, the shepherds kneel to offer homage to the new-born Child, who lies at the Virgin's feet, while the third represents the visit of the Magi.

The same freedom of brushwork characterises another "Annunciation," of probably the same time, and treated in much the same manner, although less stately than that of the Uffizi. This is one part of a *predella* formerly belonging to the Mancini Collection of Città di Castello. [54] The Archangel, with great wings half folded, and blown drapery, is just alighting at the feet of the Virgin, who has dropped her book, and drawn back with startled gesture at the impetuous rush of the messenger.

Connected with these by the same qualities of breadth of treatment, and almost modern impressionism in the conception of the scene, are two compartments of a *predella*, belonging to Mr Benson in London, representing "The Dispute by the Way," and "The Supper at Emmaus." In the former especially, the dramatic realism with which the Apostles are depicted, as they argue with animated gestures, is extraordinarily vivid. [Pg 52]

Yet another *predella* picture—"The Feast in the House of Simon," now in the Dublin Gallery—belongs approximately to this period. It is a most beautiful representation of the scene, and is treated somewhat in the gay manner of Bonifazio or Paolo Veronese. At a long table, crowded with guests, Christ sits, with His Mother on His right hand, the master of the feast being conspicuous in the middle. Over Christ's head, the Magdalen, a charming and graceful figure, pours the ointment, and on the left of the table Judas, with expressive gesture, calls attention to the waste. Notwithstanding the small size of the panel, and the number of the figures, the effect is exceedingly spacious and free. It is a well-composed scene, full of animation, and broad in treatment, and is fortunately in a good state of preservation. The altar-pieces to which all this series of *predelle* belong are unknown.

We will now consider the fine Standard, painted in 1494 for the church of Santo Spirito in Urbino. [55] On one side was represented the "Crucifixion," and on the other "The Descent of the Holy Ghost at Pentecost," but the canvases have now been divided. In the former, at the foot of the Cross is grouped the first of those characteristic scenes of the fainting Virgin which was, probably from its dramatic element, so favourite a subject with Signorelli. Sincerely and naturally felt, it in no way trenches on the melodramatic, as one or two of the later groups tend to do, and the solitary figure of Christ, raised high above the sorrowing women, is for once, among his Cruci [Pg 53] fixions, of dignity and real pathos. The solemnity of the mood given, is enhanced by the fine idea of the soldier on the left, who, impressively standing out against the sky, shades his eyes, with bewildered gesture, as though blinded by a sudden comprehension of the sacrifice. The grief of the women who tend the unconscious Virgin, is sympathetically realised, and without exaggeration of outward sorrow. The composition is specially beautiful, the sides are well-balanced, while the two mounted soldiers on either side (notwithstanding their characteristically badly-drawn horses) give the scene a ceremonious stateliness, which is very impressive.

[*Uffizi, Florence*
THE ANNUNCIATION

In the "Pentecost" we have another most masterly bit of perspective and fine spacious effect. At the end of a long room, between two rows of the Apostles, is seated the Virgin. Above is God the Father, attended by two angels, and below, the tongues of flame, the gift of the hovering Dove, have alighted on the heads of all the company. Apart from the sense of space and the well-composed grouping, the technical execution does not appear so satisfactory as in the "Crucifixion," but this may be accounted for by the fact that the painting has suffered more from restoration.

Very closely allied to this Standard in composition is the fine "S. Sebastian" of Città di Castello, painted in 1496 for the church of S. Domenico, now in the Gallery, which, in spite of its bad condition is a picture of great importance and beauty. The least satisfactory part is the Saint himself, who stands bound high up upon the tree, his sentimental face with upturned eyes [Pg 54] and open mouth recalling the S. John of several of the Crucifixions. Above him leans God the Father, and below five soldiers string their bows or shoot, with superb gestures. Three of them are in the tight-fitting clothes in which Signorelli loved to display the fine proportions and splendidly-developed muscles of his figures, and the other two are draped only with the Pollaiuolesque striped loin-cloth. In the middle distance, burgesses and sad-faced women look on at the martyrdom, and in the background a distant street, filled with soldiers, leads steeply up to a ruined classic building, not unlike the Colosseum. The great damage which the picture has suffered makes it difficult on a superficial view to give it the place it really deserves among the master's works. The colouring is somewhat crude, especially the flesh-tints, which are red and heavy, but it must nevertheless be ranked high on account of the composition, and the fine drawing and modelling of the foreground figures.

[*Santo Spirito, Urbino*

THE CRUCIFIXION

To the following year, 1487, belong the series of eight frescoes painted by Signorelli in the cloister of the Benedictine Monastery of Monte Oliveto. Vasari writes: "At Chiusuri, near Siena, the principal habitation of the monks of Monte Oliveto, he painted on one side of the cloister eleven scenes of the life and work of S. Benedict." [56] Vasari has mistaken the number of the paintings, for there were never more than nine, even supposing the last, of which only a slight fragment remains, to have been by him. To me it seems doubtful, but the fragments are in so ruined a state, the fresco having been almost entirely cut away in the [Pg 55] enlarging of the doorway, that certainty one way or the other is hardly possible. The remaining eight are for the most part in a deplorable condition, both from the damage of time and neglect, and also from repainting, the lower part of the foreground in all of them being completely lost, and smeared over with a surface of thick green. The paintings are very unequal, some being comparatively poor, while the two last are exceedingly fine. The story begins in the middle of the Saint's life. The first scene shows "How God punished Florenzo," a wicked rival abbot, who had tried to poison S. Benedict, and to lead his monks astray. In the background four grotesque devils are tearing down the walls of his convent, with extraordinary energy of action, and three others bear away the soul of the monk, whose body may be seen crushed beneath the ruins. In the foreground the Saint listens to the tale, told by a kneeling brother.

The scene is conceived in a spirit somewhat trivial for Signorelli, and has but little of his usual stately strength. The composition is too much crowded on one side, and, as far as can be judged from the state of the fresco, the draperies of the monks are mechanically treated. The parts most worthy of praise seem to be the vivacity of the devils, and the effect of spacious distance, but it is in so damaged a condition that it would be unfair to be overcritical.

The next is in an even worse condition. It illustrates "How S. Benedict converted the inhabitants of Monte Cassino," to whom, supported by two monks, he preaches in the foreground. In the middle distance others pull down from its pillar the statue of Apollo, worshipped by [Pg 56] these people. This is a very much finer painting. The composition is again overcrowded on one side, but there is much noble dignity in the figures of the three monks, and the beautiful architecture and perspective of the Temple, are admirable. The foreground has been entirely destroyed, the draperies are nearly effaced, and a little town in the background is so smeared over with green paint, that the effects of distance are lost.

No. III. is in better condition, though very much injured in the foreground. It shows "How S. Benedict exorcised the Devil upon the stone," who guarded the place where the statue of Apollo was buried, which brought a curse on the convent. In the background is seen the disinterment of the statue, and to the right, the vengeance of the Devil, who sets fire to their building. Flames burst through the windows, and the monks hasten with excited gestures to quench them. These remind one in their *naiveté* of Carpaccio's scurrying friars, in S. Giorgio degli Schiavone, Venice. There are some very fine bits in this fresco; the attitude of the monk to the left who is heaving up the stone is exceedingly good and true to nature, and the landscape is spacious and distant.

No. IV. shows "How S. Benedict resuscitated the monk upon whom the wall fell," the scene of the death taking place in the background, the Devil having precipitated him from the scaffolding on which he was at work. In the middle distance three brothers bear the dead body, and in the foreground the Saint stands and raises him again to life. This fresco is very fine both in general composition and detail. The little scene of the death is full of action and animation, the group of monks [Pg 57] who bear the corpse is dignified, and very noble is the kneeling figure of the resuscitated friar.

The paintings get gradually better, as though Signorelli had warmed to his task. The next is very charming and one of the most successful in composition. It illustrates "How S. Benedict reveals to two monks where and when they had eaten out of the Convent." The two disobedient brothers sit in the foreground of a long room (of most excellent perspective), and are served with meats and drinks. At the end of the room, at the open doorway stands the graceful figure of a youth. The section of the wall is given, showing in the distance the penitent brothers on their knees before the Saint, who has reproved their disobedience. There is something almost German in the domestic simplicity with which Signorelli has conceived the scene. The woman who waits on the right is Peruginesque in type and attitude, although with the robust physique that belongs to Signorelli. The fresco is much repainted especially in the roof.

[*Monti Oliveto, Maggiore*
MIRACLE OF S. BENEDICT

The next shows "How S. Benedict reproves the brother of the monk Valerian for his violated fast," and reveals to him that it was the Devil who had tempted him in the disguise of a traveller, the different scenes, as usual, going on in the background. In front the youth kneels before the monks, and to the right the Devil, his horns showing through his cap, tempts him. In the distance they can be seen feasting under a rock. The fresco is much injured and repainted, but the figure of the Devil with the bundle over his shoulder is very fine and well drawn.

The two last of the series are the best. Signorelli has [Pg 58] in them given the rein to his love of martial scenes, and painted them with great animation and verve. In No. VII. we have the scene "How S. Benedict discovers the deceit of Totila," and unmasks the shield-bearer, who, disguised as the King of the Goths, comes to prove the knowledge of the saint. In the background, a plain covered with camps and soldiers, Totila sends forth his servant, and in the foreground the Saint, surrounded by four monks, proclaims to him his identity. Statesmen, arrogant pages, and warriors, stand behind the exposed shield-bearer. It is interesting to observe how Signorelli's attention has wandered from the empty faces and mechanically executed draperies of the monks, and concentrated itself on this group. The figures, in their tight clothes, are superbly posed and modelled, especially the three who stand next to the shield-bearer.

The last of the frescoes is almost as fine a study of magnificent attitude. It shows "How S. Benedict recognises and welcomes Totila," the real King of the Goths, who kneels before him, surrounded by his army on horse and foot. In the background, troops are marching with great animation, (one of those fine effects of combined movement so characteristic of the master). Some of the foreground figures are again splendidly drawn and modelled, and the mounted soldiers sit their horses exceedingly well.

[*Monti Oliveto, Maggiore*
MIRACLE OF S. BENEDICT
In these two last paintings we get a hint of the great work that was to come three years later—at Orvieto. Signorelli has put forth all his strength in these groups of swaggering youths in every posture of conscious power and pride, and never perhaps been more successful in individual figures. Some of [Pg 59] the faces in the last fresco appear to be portraits, and if it be true, as Vasari says, that he painted the Vitelli and Baglioni, it is here probably that we should find them rather than among the audience of Antichrist.

In running the eye down the whole series of frescoes, the scheme of colour, as far as can be judged in their present condition, does not strike one as pleasant. Crude blues, emerald greens, brownish purples, heavy earthen browns—these are the predominating tints. The flesh tones are uniformly red and heavy. Neither is the decorative effect of the compositions specially good, as at Loreto, and more particularly at Orvieto. Perhaps even, on a superficial view, the space-filling by Sodoma is happier, and has a more imposing effect. It is chiefly in detail that the great qualities of Signorelli show themselves.

The rest of the walls of the large cloister are painted with twenty-seven subjects by Sodoma, showing the youth and hermit-life of the saint, and continuing, after the series by Signorelli, with his miracles and his old age. Although the subjects chosen by Luca illustrate the later years, yet they were painted first, and it is probable that the place of each scene was arranged before any of the work was entered upon.

The year following the execution of these frescoes Signorelli was in Siena, painting the two wings for the altar-piece of the Bicchi family, formerly in the church of S. Agostino, now in the Berlin Gallery, No. 79. A MS. of the Abbate Galgano Bicchi, [Pg 60] which gives the date, speaks of it as an *Ancona*, the centre of which was a statue of S. Christopher by Jacopo della Quercia, and with a *predella*, which the Abbate minutely describes. [57] Nothing now

remains of the altar-piece but these two beautiful wings, one of which contains figures of the Magdalen, Santa Chiara, and S. Jerome, the other, of S. Augustine, S. Antonio and S. Catherine of Siena. Vasari writes of it: "At Siena he painted in Sant'Agostino, a picture for the chapel of S. Cristofano, in which are some Saints surrounding a S. Christopher in relief." [58]

Both panels are of very rich and harmonious colour, especially the one containing the noble figure of the Magdalen, in her green robe shot with gold and deep red mantle, and her ropes of honey-coloured hair.

[*Gallery, Berlin*
SAINTS
Perhaps about the same date, perhaps somewhat earlier, we may place the fine *Tondo* (No. 79B) hanging in the same gallery, formerly in the Patrizi collection, Rome. I have not given it its usual name of a "Visitation," because that scene, conventionally treated, took place before the birth of the children who here play so important a part. Signorelli has, according to his habit, conceived the subject without any reference

to traditional custom. I have already spoken of the ease with which he composes in the *Tondo* form, and this is perhaps the best example of his skill. The natural grouping of the figures, the sweeping curves of the draperies, which, especially that of S. Joseph accentuated with gold, carry out the lines [Pg 61] of the circle, give a sense of rest and harmony to the eye. The scene is treated with a simplicity and noble dignity which deserve special praise. It is in some ways the most sympathetic of all his Holy Families, and he seems to have felt the charm of every-day simple life, and for once has given the Christ the life and beauty of childhood. The tender foreboding sadness in the face of the Virgin, the reverential sympathy of the aged Elizabeth, and the kindly care with which the powerful Zacharias holds the Child, are touches full of poetry.

Morelli places this *Tondo* as a late work, [59] but the soft and harmonious colour, as well as the poetic feeling, seem to belong to this period, before the painting of the Orvieto frescoes, if not even earlier.

[*Gallery, Berlin*
HOLY FAMILY
(CALLED VISITATION)

Lastly, in this group must be placed the Standard of Borgo San Sepolcro, painted for the Confraternity S. Antonio Abbate, now in the Municipio. It is interesting to note, as its position in the Gallery allows us to do, how completely Signorelli has now detached himself from the influence of his first master— outwardly at least. No greater contrast could well be, than the unrestful dramatic realism of the "Crucifixion" on this Standard, and the inspired serenity of the "Resurrection" of Pier dei Franceschi close by; than the coarsely-conceived figure of the crucified Christ, with its heavy features and uncouth limbs, and the spiritual beauty of the risen Saviour.

This "Crucifixion" is the least successful of all Signorelli's renderings of this subject (with the exception, perhaps, of the Morra fresco), both from [Pg 62] its technical defects of extreme hardness and heavy colour, as well as from the lack of any real feeling in the painter for his subject. The unfortunate introduction of the patron saint, posing as Joseph of Arimathœa, disturbs the harmony of the mood, while his exaggerated gesture contrasts disagreeably with the apathetic coldness of the other figures, over-dramatic as their action is. The Christ is treated deliberately as a study of muscle, and is among the most ignominious of his types, and the fantastic landscape, with its shadowy rocks and solid clouds, is badly composed and without existence. Although there is no trace of the influence of Piero remaining, yet there is much of Antonio Pollaiuolo, especially in the muscular figure and bent legs of the Christ.

[*Municipio, Borgo San Sepolcro*
THE CRUCIFIXION

The two large Saints on the reverse of the Standard are, on the other hand, imposing and noble figures, splendidly painted in Signorelli's grandest and most sweeping manner. S. Antonio, in the black habit of the order for which the banner was executed, stands reading in a book, and by his side is S. Eligio, the smith-saint, in red mantle and dark-green robe, holding in one hand the farrier's tool, and in the other the cut-off horse's hoof of the legend. Below kneel small figures of four brothers of the Confraternity.

We have now come to the end of the series of works, executed, as nearly as can be judged, between 1490 and 1499, and with the latter date have arrived at the time of the painting of the Orvieto frescoes, which were to be the crowning point in the life's work of the master.

FOOTNOTES:

[53] "Purg." ii. 37 and 35.
[54] When last heard of by the author it was for sale in England.
[55] The contract, dated June 1494, is transcribed in Pungileoni's "Elogio Stor. di Giov. Santi," p. 77.
[56] Vasari, iii. 689.
[57] The MS. is in the possession of Conte Scipione Bicchi-Borghese, Siena.
[58] Vasari, iii. 688.
[59] "Die Galerie zu Berlin," p. 46.
[Pg 63]

CHAPTER V

ORVIETO

There seems to be a moment in the life of every great man in which he touches the height of his possibilities, and reaches the limits of his powers of expression. To Signorelli it came late, at an age when most men begin to feel at least their physical powers on the wane. The two last frescoes of the Monte Oliveto series indicate that an immense force lay in reserve, waiting an opportunity for some wider and freer field of action, than had hitherto presented itself. That opportunity now came, when, at the age of fifty-nine, he was called upon to undertake the vast work of these Orvieto frescoes. With the exception of the Sistine Chapel, no such task has been achieved at so sustained a pitch of imaginative power and technical excellence. Whether the subject stirred his dramatic spirit, or whether the great spaces to be filled gave an expanded sense of liberty to his genius, or whether his powers, intellectual and physical, really were at the zenith of their strength; whatever was the cause, he succeeded in executing a work which ranks among the greatest monuments of the Renaissance, perhaps should even rank as the very greatest.

Morelli writes: "These masterpieces appear to me unequalled in the art of the fifteenth century; for to [Pg 64] no other contemporary painter was it given to endow the human frame with a like degree of passion, vehemence, and strength." [60] And beside the dignity with which he has in these frescoes elevated the body to an almost superhuman grandeur, his conception of supernatural things is proportionately solemn and impressive. It is impossible to look at the scenes without emotion, and the mood evoked is due in a great measure to the earnest conviction with which they are conceived. Signorelli, always a religious painter, in the wider meaning of the word, seems here to assume an almost prophetic attitude of warning, embodied, one might almost think, in the portrait of himself, stern and menacing, standing sentinel-like over the work.

Vasari thus speaks of the frescoes: "In the principal church of Orvieto—that of the Madonna—he completed with his own hand the chapel which had been begun there by Fra Giovane da Fiesole; in which he painted all the history of the end of the world, with strange fantastic invention: Angels, demons, ruins, earthquakes, fires, miracles of Antichrist, and many other of the like things; besides which, nudes, foreshortened figures, and many beautiful designs; having pictured to himself the terror which will be in that latest tremendous day. By means of this he roused the spirit of all those who came after him in such a way that since, they have found the difficulty of that manner easy. Wherefore it does not surprise me that the works of Luca should have always been most highly praised by Michelagnolo, nor that certain things of his divine Judgement which [Pg 65] he painted in the chapel were in part courteously taken from the invention of Luca; as are the Angels, Demons, the heavenly orders, and other things in which Michelagnolo imitated the style of Luca, as everyone may see. Luca portrayed in the above-mentioned work himself and many of his friends; Niccolò, Paulo and Vitellozzo Vitelli; Giovan, Paulo and Orazio Baglioni, and others whose names are unknown. " [61]

[*Cathedral, Orvieto*
PORTRAITS OF SIGNORELLI AND FRA ANGELICO
(DETAIL FROM ANTICHRIST)

Fifty-two years before, in 1447, Fra Angelico had spent three months and a half in this Cathedral of Orvieto, painting the spandrels in the roof of the Cappella Nuova, as it was then called. [62] He had time to complete only two frescoes, being either recalled to Rome by Nicholas V., or to the convent of S. Domenico, near Fiesole (of which, in 1450, he was made Prior). These two works are among the best and strongest of his paintings. In the principal space, that over the altar, he painted Christ in glory, surrounded by a *mandorla*, with angels on either side; and in the spandrel on the right, a group of sixteen prophets, seated pyramidally against a blaze of gold background. It is probable that he had thought out the general scheme of the frescoes, and that Signorelli only carried out his intention in working the paintings into one great whole—Christ in Heaven, surrounded by Angels, Apostles, Martyrs, Virgins, Patriarchs and Fathers of the Church, witnessing from on high the execution of divine justice below. However that may be, it is [Pg 66] certain that Signorelli, in his painting of the roof, kept most scrupulously to the older master's arrangement, and in one of the spandrels actually seems to have worked over his design.

After the withdrawal of Fra Angelico, the chapel remained untouched for more than fifty years. In 1449 his pupil, Benozzo Gozzoli, who had probably been his assistant in the painting, demanded permission to continue the work; but the authorities were not content to grant it, and it was only in 1499, after some futile negotiations with Perugino, who appears to have refused the commission, that they finally resolved to place the decoration in the hands of Signorelli. Perhaps decided to this step by the success of the Monte Oliveto frescoes, they were yet so cautious and so determined to have only the very best work in their chapel, that at first they only entrusted to him the painting of the vaulting, already begun. They were wise to be careful in their choice, for they were probably conscious of the extreme beauty of their cathedral, and, in particular, of the exquisite architecture of this chapel. Orvieto Cathedral is one of the finest and most impressive of the Italian churches, and from its foundation in 1290, the authorities had been notoriously lavish in their expenditure for its building, and fastidious in their choice of architects, sculptors, and painters. [63] From the point of view merely of decoration, they could have given the work to no better artist than Signorelli, and the first impression, on passing into the chapel from the austere and [Pg 67] spacious nave, is of the harmonious plan, both of colour and design, with which the original beauty of the architecture has been enhanced, and its graceful characteristics accentuated.

The roof is of very perfect shape, and

the spaces well adapted for painting. It is divided in the middle by an arch, thus having two complete vaultings, each with four spandrels. The walls are high and spacious, also divided in two parts, in each of which, on either side, is a large fresco. Signorelli has separated the lower part of the wall by a painted frieze of delicate gold and ivory, and in the lower half executed a series of portraits, each surrounded by medallions in *grisaille*, containing small subject-pictures, the rest of the space being filled with an intricate pattern of grotesques. The south wall, in which are three small windows, has been unfortunately disfigured by a *baroque* seventeenth-century altar, whose projections hide a part of the frescoes. Opposite is the entrance, a magnificently-proportioned portal, with a rounded arch, most delicately decorated in colour. Every inch of the walls is covered, and for the most part by the work of Signorelli himself, the above-mentioned grotesques, the merely ornamental painting, and a few of the medallions alone being by his assistants.

In describing the frescoes I intend to begin with those of the vaulting, and then to work gradually round the walls from the left of the entrance, where the first of the series of larger paintings begins with "The Preaching and Fall of Antichrist."

In the spandrel opposite the Christ of Fra Angelico, Signorelli has painted eight angels holding the symbols [Pg 68] of the Passion, while two others, not unlike the great Archangels of the "Resurrection," blow trumpets to announce the impending Judgment.

Left of the altar, opposite Fra Angelico's "Prophets," and arranged in exactly the same pyramidal form, is a magnificent group, representing the "Apostles," the Virgin being seated on the lowest tier with S. Peter and S. Paul. Very noble, impressive figures, powerfully and solidly painted, with broadly-draped, heavy-folded robes, they sit like rocks upon clouds as solid as hills.

These, with the two frescoes of Fra Angelico, complete the paintings of the first vaulting.

Those on the other side of the arch are executed entirely by Signorelli, and, with the exception of one, from his own designs. This one is the weakest of his roof-paintings in execution, and the composition and actual drawing of the central figures, are the work of Fra Angelico. It represents the "Choir of Martyrs," a group of seven figures. In the centre are seated three Deacons in full canonicals, with Bishops on either side, and below two Saints in plain robes. These last have all Signorelli's characteristics of drawing, and sit with widespread knees and broadly-painted draperies, a striking contrast to the weak attitudes and niggling robes of the central group. Signorelli has indeed hardly altered the childish chubby features of the Deacon in the middle, nor the benevolent vacuity of the two Bishops, so different to his own austere types.

Opposite to this, over the portal, is a group of eight "Virgins," broadly and vigorously treated, in Signorelli's [Pg 69] boldest manner. To the right is another of the pyramidal groups, fifteen "Doctors of the Church," some of whom are represented disputing and discussing points of theology.

The last of the roof-paintings is a powerful group of "Patriarchs," ranking, with that of the "Apostles," among the most impressive of the frescoes. Here appear many of his well-known types of face; the melancholy features of Pan are repeated in the turbaned youth in the top row, intended perhaps to be Solomon; the Christ of the Uffizi "Holy Family" is in the second tier to the left; the powerful Zacharias from the Berlin *Tondo* in the lowest.

Luzi, in his minute description of the paintings, [64] has bestowed names on all these figures, without much advantage, since they are for the most part doubtful. Few of them bear symbols, but the different groups are sufficiently described in large letters, by the painters themselves— GLORIOSVS APOSTOLORVM CHOIR—MARTIRVM CANDIDATVS EXERCITVS —etc. etc.

The figures, with the exception of those by Fra Angelico, and the design for the "Martyrs," are entirely the work of Signorelli himself. The decorations between the spaces seem to be in part by the assistant of Fra Angelico—perhaps Benozzo Gozzoli. In the first border heads are painted, in lozenges, at regular intervals, a few of which are in the older master's style, while many show the manner of Signorelli. The rounded projecting rib is painted with foliage of cypress-green, with here and there rich red and golden flowers gleaming out, and on either side a border of [Pg 70] conventionalised water-lilies. It is difficult to say which of the masters designed this exceedingly beautiful decoration, but it is most effective, and well-calculated to accentuate the life of the fine curves in the vaulting.

[*Cathedral, Orvieto*
PATRIARCHS

These groups of Signorelli's are noble and impressive paintings, in technique strong and vigorous. The draperies are treated with simplicity and breadth of fold, and the gold background gives richness and beauty to the colour. No wonder that the authorities, jealous though they were at the beauty of their chapel, should have hesitated no longer to hand over the great spaces of the walls to the brush of the painter who had so well executed their first commission.

In the April of the following year, 1500, the new task was given. The payment for the roof was to have been 205 ducats; for the walls they offered 575. Besides this, the painter was to be furnished with ultramarine, a certain quantity of food and wine, and a free lodging, with two beds, as the lengthy documents of commission minutely tell. [65]

The paintings begin with "The Preaching and Fall of Antichrist." Here the foreground is filled with groups of the followers of the false prophet, who, with the features of Christ, stands on a little raised dais, listening with an evil expression, as the Devil behind him, unseen by the crowd, whispers into his ear what he shall say. Before the dais are scattered gold vessels, bars and coins, with which he tempts the audience. Farther back to the right, different groups represent [Pg 71] the false teaching and miracles of Antichrist, and in the background is his Temple, with armed men going in and out of its open portico. The left of the frescoes is devoted to the fall of the false prophet, and the destruction of his followers. Above we see him precipitated head-downwards from heaven by an angel surrounded by fiery rays, which strike death to the army beneath.

[*Cathedral, Orvieto*
THE PREACHING AND FALL OF ANTICHRIST
In sombre black, and standing outside the scene, Signorelli has painted the portrait of himself, with fingers interlaced and firmly-planted feet, and behind, the milder, but still gloomy figure of Fra Angelico.

There is something sinister in the saturnine melancholy on the faces of the crowd, unrelieved by any lightness, and culminating in the evil expression of Antichrist himself. The peace of the gold-flecked landscape only accentuates the horror of the scene of the downfall in the background. The picture is a fit prologue to the terrible Judgment to come.

In composition the fresco is very fine, the values of distance are well kept, and the meaning of the scene is obvious and significant, and dramatically rendered. The foreground group is very strongly painted, natural in attitude and gesture, and the figure of a man in striped hose is magnificently modelled. I do not care to touch on so hypothetical a thing as the supposed portraiture in this group, but it is interesting to note, in the old man right of Antichrist, the features familiar to us in the drawings of Leonardo, possibly painted from a study of the same model. Behind is a profile head, obviously intended for Dante. The terrible force of the angel, with its [Pg 72] hawk-like swoop, the unresisting heavy fall of the body through the air, are rendered with extraordinary power. The foreshortening is admirable, and so is the fine perspective of the beautiful architecture of the Temple.

The figures of the soldiers on the steps recall Perugino in the manner of treatment—dark against light, and well detached from the background. The capitals of the pillars, the buttons on the clothes, and the rays of the angel are embossed with gilded gesso, as also are the distant hills. This form of ornamentation, so much used by Signorelli in these frescoes, adds greatly to their decorative beauty.

Under this painting is a square-shaped portrait, half cut away by a recess, in which stands a modern altar. It is supposed by Luzi to represent Homer, and is the first of a series which run all round the walls, much repainted, but all of them the work of the master himself. They are surrounded by four medallions, painted in *grisaille*, also for the most part by Signorelli, but in this case only two, and a fragment of the third, remain, the enlarging of the recess having almost entirely cut that and the fourth away. In the top medallion are five nude figures, a powerful female and four males, all wildly hastening as if from some impending destruction. In that on the left a a man stands on a dais, surrounded by soldiers who hold a prisoner bound before him. In the lower fragment, only one figure remains. These all represent, according to Luzi, scenes from Homer. The groups are well composed and full of vigorous energy, the nudes are splendidly modelled in broad, bold strokes, [Pg 73] so sharply drawn on the wet plaster that the outlines are deeply incised. Where, as here, these *grisaille* pictures are the work of Signorelli himself, they are worthy of more attention than is usually given to them, being as fine as any of his best work. To realise fully their vigour and excellence, one need only compare these powerful nudes with those painted in the pilasters close by, the work of assistants. The medallions in every case are surrounded by a broadly painted coloured pattern of grotesques, also by assistants, but probably to a large extent designed by Signorelli, for they are extremely characteristic of his preoccupation with the human form and with movement. Arabesques have but little attraction for him, and it will be noticed that in all his ornamental work where it is possible, he paints figures. These decorations are almost entirely composed of fantastic creatures, fauns, tiny satyrs, horses, birds, etc., who blending their shapes and borrowing each other's limbs, frisk all over the walls, and by their gambols and contortions form a pattern of curves and lines, which is a maze of animated life, retaining at the same time the broad and harmonious effect of an arabesque.

[*Cathedral, Orvieto*
THE CROWNING OF THE ELECT
The next large painting represents "The Crowning of the Elect." A crowd of men and women, many draped round the loins, some quite naked, gaze upwards ecstatically, or kneel reverently

to receive the gold crowns which angels are placing on their heads. Above, seated on clouds, are nine other angels, draped in many-folded robes, who play musical instruments. To the right two figures (in one of whom the Echo [Pg 74] of the "Pan" is repeated) seem to walk out of the scene, thus connecting this fresco with the next, in which the elect and crowned souls prepare to ascend to Heaven.

The background is entirely of gold, thickly studded with bosses of gilded gesso. The figures are finely modelled and posed. The flesh-painting, as in all the frescoes, is perhaps somewhat heavy in colour, but the whole effect is rich and harmonious. The chief defects in the work are the overcrowding of the composition, and the bad values of distance, caused in a great measure by the gold background. Signorelli's treatment is too realistic, his figures are too solid and too true to life, to bear the decorative background so suitable to the flat, half-symbolic painting of the Sienese school. They need space and air behind them, and lacking that, one feels a disagreeable sensation of oppression and overcrowding. Keeping the eye upon the ground, which is treated naturally, this feeling goes; the long shadows distinctly marked, send the figures to their different planes, and the confused composition becomes clear.

Underneath are the usual decorations, two square portraits surrounded each by four medallions. We do not need the help of Luzi to recognise Dante in the first, injured though it is, and much repainted, especially about the mouth, which gives the face a somewhat grotesque expression.

[*Cathedral, Orvieto*
SUBJECTS FROM DANTE
The *grisaille* paintings represent stories from the "Purgatorio," but although fine in design, are not executed by Signorelli himself. They have none of the breadth and grandeur of the first series, and the [Pg 75] effect is meagre and niggling, equal importance being given to the rocks and to the figures.

The other portrait is probably intend-

ed for Virgil, who, with upturned face and melodramatic expression, seems to seek for inspiration. This expression is exaggerated, but the painting is vigorous and strong.

Around, the medallions again represent subjects from the "Purgatorio," and are apparently by the same hand as the last, with the exception of the lower one, which seems to have some of Signorelli's own work in the nude figures.

The south wall is pierced by three lancet windows, the central one over the altar, dividing the two principal frescoes of "Heaven" and "Hell." The former is, as I have said, a continuation of the last scene, and represents angels preceding the elect souls, and showing them the way to Heaven. In the sky, heavily embossed with gold like the last, float angels with musical instruments, one of whom, with face downward, blowing a pipe, is not so successfully foreshortened as is usual with Signorelli.

[*Cathedral, Orvieto*
HEAVEN
In the thickness of the small window which cuts into this fresco, are painted two coloured medallions, one of an angel vanquishing a devil, the other of S. Michael, with the balances, weighing souls—both by the master himself. Below are two series of small pictures in *grisaille*, with scenes from the "Purgatorio." The lowest is unfortunately hidden by the altar. All of them are by Signorelli himself, exceedingly good, and worthy of careful study, one being especially beautiful—the top picture of the first series, in which Dante and Virgil stand before the Angel, with the gold-plumed Eagle [Pg 76] in the foreground—a most nobly conceived illustration to the ninth canto of the "Purgatorio."

[*Cathedral, Orvieto*
HELL
On the opposite side of the altar is the Judgment of Minos, and the driving of the lost souls to Hell under the superintendence of the two Archangels, who stand in the sky with drawn swords, sorrowfully watching the fulfilment of di-

vine justice. Signorelli here has followed very closely the text of the "Inferno." In the foreground "Minos standeth horribly and gnasheth," condemning the miserable souls before him each to his different circle, his tail wound twice about his middle. Farther back, the Pistoiese, Vanno Fucci, with blasphemous gesture, yells out his challenge to God; Charon plies his boat; and in the background despairing souls follow a mocking demon who runs before them with a banner.

The two medallions on the sides of the window contain, one the Archangel Gabriel with the lily of the Annunciation, the other a very beautiful group of Raphael and Tobias, both by Signorelli himself. Below, the decorations correspond to those on the opposite side, the *grisaille* pictures, representing, according to Luzi, scenes from the "Metamorphoses" of Ovid, all, with the exception, perhaps, of the medallion just below the window, being also the work of the master, and very powerfully painted.

Leaving the window wall, we now come to the finest of all the frescoes, the magnificent scene of the "Damnation." So vivid is the realisation, so lifelike the movements and gestures, that the writhing mass appears really alive, and one can almost hear the horrible clamour of the devils, and the despairing yells [Pg 77] of the victims. The general effect is of one simultaneous convulsed movement, one seething turmoil. In detail, the horror is most dramatically rendered. The malignancy of the devils, their brutal fury as they claw their prey, tear at their throats, and wrench back their heads; the utter horror and anguish of the victims, the confusion, the uproar, are given with a convincing realistic force, which makes the scene ghastly and terrible. In most representations of Hell, and especially of Devils, human imagination fails in conveying any sense of real horror, even the earnest Dürer and Botticelli treating them with a grotesqueness which shows how far they were from any conviction of their reality. Signorelli is the only painter of the Renaissance I can recall who has succeeded in giving a savage sternness, a formidable brutishness to his fiends, which is very far from grotesque, but is really appalling. These ferocious creatures are of all colours, slate-blue, crude purple, heavy green, livid mauve—sometimes of all these poisonous-looking colours fading one into the other. Strong and malevolent, they triumph in their work of torture, with a gloomy malignancy very different from the trifling malice of the fiends he painted at Monte Oliveto. Above stand the three Archangels, in armour, with half-drawn swords, menacing those who try to fly upward instead of toward the flames of Hell. Two, in their hurry to escape chastisement, let fall their prey; another, with great bat-wings which cut the air like scythes, swoops down again into the chaos below.

[*Cathedral, Orvieto*
THE DAMNATION

I suppose a mass of convulsed limbs has never been rendered in so masterly a manner. The effect is so [Pg 78] natural that one is inclined to forget the difficulties Signorelli has so superbly overcome. But if one considers in detail the different attitudes, the violent action of the arms and legs, the contorted positions of the bodies—every muscle either on the stretch or relaxed into a flaccid limpness,—the foreshortened limbs twisted into every kind of unnatural posture, and the complicated interweaving of the whole, one realises that it is indeed his masterpiece, not only for the mood of terror and awe it induces by its imaginative power, but for its marvellous rendering of tumultuous movement, and the ease with which enormous technical difficulties have been surmounted.

The portraits below are, according to Luzi, of Ovid and Horace, the four medallions round the former seeming, in their energy and furious life, to carry out the tumult of the great fresco above. They represent scenes from "The Metamorphoses," and deal chiefly with Hades and the infernal Deities. Above stand four female figures with fluttering draperies, among whom we can distinguish Diana with the bow, and Pallas with the lance and shield. Below, Pluto stands in a chariot drawn by dragons. This painting is very much injured, as is much of this lower part of the wall, especially the grotesques. On the right Pluto bears away Persephone in his arms in a chariot drawn by two fantastic horses, which an attendant urges furiously forward with a caduceus. On the left Ceres, with wildly-floating hair, leaps into a tearing chariot drawn by two winged serpents, which Cupid goads onward with a flaming torch. These are all by Signorelli himself, and, for the rendering of violent [Pg 79] movement, worthy of their position under the great painting.

Round the other portrait are subjects also connected with the infernal regions. Over it, Æneas stands before the Cumœan Sybil, a very injured painting. Below, Orpheus in Hades plays before Pluto and Persephone to win back Eurydice, who lies bound before them. On the right Hercules rescues Theseus from Hades, and slays Cerberus, and on the left, Eurydice, following Orpheus, looks back, and is re-seized by the demons. These are all exceedingly good and dramatic paintings, and are by Signorelli himself.

The next large space, after the fresco of "The Damnation," is filled with "The Resurrection." Above, the two mighty Archangels sound their trumpets, and the dead wake, and break through the crust of the grey earth below. They stand about embracing each other, or helping each other to rise, or gazing with rapture up at the Archangels, who, with fluttering draperies and ribbons, and great spread wings of purple and peacock-green, stand, surrounded by little shadowy cherubs, in the gold-embossed sky. Most of the figures are of Signorelli's usual powerful build, one, however, is an emaciated youth with little on his bones but skin, many are skeletons. To these last he has given a pathetic look of ecstasy, which is wonderfully expressive, considering it is obtained only by means of eyeless sockets and grinning jaw-bones.

[*Cathedral, Orvieto*
THE RESURRECTION

The fresco has suffered much, particularly from the painting, in later times, of draperies round the loins, some of which have been worn or rubbed half off. [Pg 80] Almost in the centre is a large stain, outlining the shape of a window, which Signorelli caused to be filled up, and which can still be seen on the outside of the Cathedral. The damp, oozing through the new plaster round the framework, partly destroyed the painting, but the centre is remarkably well preserved.

It is interesting to note in studying this fresco, that, student of anatomy though he was, the skeleton seems to have had little attraction for Signorelli. The placing of the bones is, of course, correct, but the delicacy of their curves, their relative proportions and thicknesses, their beauty of detail, are not given at all. For example, in the skeleton in the foreground, the pelvis has scarcely the shape, and none of the variety of line, of the bone itself, but is merely a coarsely-drawn girdle. Compared to the extreme delicacy with which he models flesh, and his minute appreciation of every gradation of curve in the muscles, this carelessness in the treatment of the skeleton is noteworthy.

Under this, the last of the larger frescoes, is a recess, in which was formerly the sarcophagus containing the bones of Pietro Parens, the patron saint of Orvieto. In this recess, under the brackets on which the sarcophagus stood, Signorelli has painted one of his most beautiful "Pietàs." Unfortunately, half hidden by a marble group, sculptured in 1574 by Ippolito Scalza, it is difficult to see, and impossible to photograph, and is therefore not so well known and appreciated as it deserves to be. The Christ is an exact repetition of the figure in the "Deposition," of the Cortona Cathedral, and was probably painted [Pg 81] about the same time—1502. The position only is reversed. The other two figures are also repeated from that altar-piece, with only very slight variations. Behind is painted the Tomb, on which is a relief in *grisaille* of four naked figures bearing the dead body of the Saviour. This formed the lower part of the now removed sarcophagus, the three stone supports of which still project from the wall. On the right of the "Pietà," is painted the martyr Pietro Parens himself. The saint gazes down with tender reverence at the scene at his feet, standing in fur-trimmed robes and cap, one hand on his breast, the other holding the palm of martyrdom. Over his head is the hammer, the instrument of his death. The face is of extreme beauty, with gentle expression, the robes are finely draped, the attitude most natural, and the whole figure is one of the noblest and most sympathetic of all Signorelli's works, and deserves to be better known. On the other side, and also as supporter of the "Pietà," stands Faustinus, another patron saint of the city, also a very beautiful figure, with features which recall the type generally used by Signorelli for S. John. At his feet lies the millstone with which he was drowned. On either side, in the thickness of the wall, is a medallion in *grisaille*, containing the scenes of their deaths, very powerfully painted.

This recess occupies more than one half of the space below "The Resurrection," allowing room for only one portrait and two medallions. The former Luzi has decided to be Lucan, and represents a beautiful youth, with a mass of loose curling hair crowned with oak-leaves and acorns. The scenes of the medallions [Pg 82] are supposed to be from "The Phaisalia." In that above three nude men fight with fists, one binds his prostrate foe, and another bears off a slain body. In that on the right four men fight with clubs and swords. All are powerful figures, painted by Signorelli in his most characteristic manner. Below the portrait of the poet is an inscription of 1667, honouring the memory of Signorelli, and of Ippolito Scalza, the sculptor of the marble "Pietà."

The frescoes round the beautifully-proportioned entrance portal, being on an inside wall, are in a state of better preservation than the rest, and the colours brighter. They represent "The Signs of the Destruction of the World." For imaginative power they can be compared only with the woodcuts of Albrecht Dürer's "Apocalypse." To our right on entering, the "Rain of Fire" shoots in heavy lines from the hands and bodies of demons with outspread wings. The distraction of the people on whom it falls is well rendered. In the foreground armed men on horse and foot seek wildly to escape the shafts, which have already precipitated some to the ground. In the middle distance the flames pursue a flying mob of terrified women clutching their infants, and men trying to protect them; while in the foreground old men, youths, and children, are struck down in heaps, stopping their ears, and gazing up in panic at the unearthly apparition.

On the opposite side the sun and moon are eclipsed, and a dark rain of blood falls from the gloomy sky. An earthquake has shaken the city, and its buildings totter and fall in fragments on the people. In the foreground is a group, perhaps intended for the [Pg 83] Prophets of the Destruction, who gaze up, less terrified, but with fear and solemn awe.

[*Cathedral, Orvieto*
SIGNS OF DESTRUCTION

Next to "The Damnation," these are perhaps the finest of the series, and show most imagination and dramatic feeling. The foreshortening of some of the figures is admirable, the composition in the restricted space is good, and there is superb drawing and modelling in the foreground figure among the Prophets in the last fresco.

In the centre, over the arch, Signorelli has painted a group of winged children, who hold a tablet by a bunch of ribbons, in one of whom are repeated the features of the Christ-child of the Uffizi "Holy Family."

In the space under "The Rain of Fire" has been painted a portrait, but not a fragment of the face remains, an obelisk-shaped monument having in later times been placed against the wall, completely destroying it. Cavalcaselle, for what reason is not clear to me, supposes that it represented Niccolò Franceschi, the treasurer of the works. On the opposite side of the doorway is a coloured medallion, representing a man with a turban, who, leaning his back over the frame as though it were a window, seems to be gazing up at the painting above. This, Cavalcaselle suggests, is a portrait of the painter himself; Luzi, however, considers it to be Empedocles. Over it in the decorations are two small tablets bearing the master's initials, L. and S.

We began by considering the general impression of the frescoes upon the mind, their great imaginative qualities, and the solemn mood they induce. We will conclude by summing up the technical excellences, which distinguish them from all his previous work by [Pg 84] extra power and ability. The beauty of the compositions, the filling of the spaces and the effectiveness of the scheme of decoration are as much above the work of three years before—the Mount Oliveto series—as is the freedom and dramatic power with which the scenes are rendered.

What chiefly strikes one is the homogeneousness of the whole design, each part of the work keeping its due place in the great scheme. We are never unconscious, even while carried away by the emotions of each separate scene, of the solemn presence of the Judges above, who preside over the final justice. Considered as subject-pictures, the intense dramatic feeling makes them extremely powerful in their different effects, so that it is impossible to look at them unmoved. Finally, the facility and freedom with which his anatomical knowledge has allowed Signorelli to render all the possibilities of movement and gesture, is as much in advance of his age, as is his modern and natural visualisation, and the impressionistic breadth of his brushwork. In that respect, indeed, it is impossible to go farther. Later painters have erred as much in exaggerating violent action and over-developing muscles, as the earlier master fell short in dry and laborious stiffness. Signorelli, while retaining the earnest sincerity and thoughtfulness of the earlier workers, has been able at the same time to render with modern facility every movement of the human frame, and the result is an achievement which no later skill has surpassed, which is perhaps the last word in the treatment of the nude in action.

Before closing these remarks, I must not omit to [Pg 85] record the gratitude due to the two German painters, Bothe and Pfannenschmidt of Würtemburg, who, in 1845, at their own cost, cleaned and carefully restored the frescoes, a work done on the whole with great discretion.

Two other paintings of the master, now in the Opera del Duomo, are so closely connected with the chapel, that the description would be incomplete without mention of them here—the altar-piece of the Magdalen, and the portraits of himself and the treasurer of the Cathedral, Niccolò Franceschi.

The former, painted originally for the Cathedral, is a life-sized, very broadly painted figure, somewhat coarse in execution, but exceedingly powerful. She wears a gorgeous gold garment, elaborately embroidered, and over it a brownish-red mantle lined with green. There is a stately dignity in the picture itself which the photograph unfortunately does not reproduce. It is dated 1504, and on the old frame is the following Inscription:

CECCARELLEVS . DE . APVIDVTIS—ET . RVFINVS .
ANTONII . —
CONSERVAT . PA . PACIS . CONSERVATRICI . EX . SE .
CONSVLTO . M.D.IIII.

The double portrait, painted in 1503, [66] is a work of the greatest importance, both by reason of the interest attached to the portraiture, and also that it remains to us absolutely untouched, every stroke being in the [Pg 86] original state as the master left it. The heads are full of character and life, powerfully and rapidly painted in black and red, on a brick or tile, thickly overlaid with gesso. The brush-strokes are bold and firm, and the outline slightly incised in the plaster. Under each head Signorelli has painted the names LVCA and NICOLAVS , and on the back is a most interesting inscription, apparently painted by himself, although the words are most probably the composition of the Treasurer. The following is a translation: "Luca Signorelli, an Italian by race, citizen of Cortona, renowned for his skill as a painter, comparable to Apelles for attainment, has, under the rule and in the pay of Niccolò Franceschi, of the same race, but a citizen of Orvieto, Treasurer of the vestry of its Cathedral, painted with clear meaning this chapel, dedicated to the Virgin, with figures of the Last Judgment; and, eager for immortal fame, on the back of this inscription, has painted the effigy of both, life-like, and with wonderful art. In the reign of Pope Alexander VI. and of the Emperor Maximilian IV. in the year of grace M.CCC-CC. in the third Kalends of January."

FOOTNOTES:

[60] "Italian Painters," i. 92.

[61] Vasari, iii. 690.

[62] It was not till the seventeenth century that the chapel was dedicated to the Madonna di San Brizio, on account of a Byzantine miraculous picture of the Virgin, still on the altar.

[63] For an account of the Cathedral, see the Padre della Valle's "Storia del Duomo di Orvieto."

[64] "Il Duomo di Orvieto." Ludovico Luzi. Firenze. Le Monnier, 1866.

[65] Preserved among the Archives of the Cathedral. Transcribed by Vischer, p. 349, etc.

[66] The head of Luca is reproduced, divided from the other, as the frontispiece.

[Pg 87]

CHAPTER VI

LATER PAINTINGS

We have seen that during the four years and a half in which Signorelli was engaged on the great work of the Orvieto frescoes, he yet spent some part of the time in his native city, and there, in 1502, he painted the signed and dated "Deposition" with its *predelle* for the church of Santa Margherita, now removed to the Cathedral. Vasari thus speaks of it: "In Santa Margherita of Cortona, his native town, belonging to the Frati del Zoccolo, he painted a dead Christ; one of his most excellent works." [67] This dead Christ is the figure which by its realism and pathos gave rise to the legend, already quoted, [68] that it was painted from the body of his own son. It is an exact counterpart of the "Pietà" in the Orvieto frescoes, except that it is here reversed. It is a work of great beauty and feeling, painted with sincere emotion, and has none of the academic dryness with which he treated the same subject in Borgo San Sepolcro. The fine grouping, the restraint with which the sorrow is rendered, the real pathos of the scene, give the picture dignity and solemnity, and the glow of colour, obtained by the lavish use of gold [Pg 88] in the embroideries, add to its richness and decorative beauty. The Virgin is nearly the same figure as in the Orvieto fresco, and in feature recalls the San Sepolcro "Crucifixion," and the Magdalen is almost identical with the altar-piece of the Opera del Duomo, just considered, although here painted with more refinement and grace. In the background is one of those vivid scenes of crowded movement, which occur so often at this period of the master's development—a group of excited soldiers pressing round the Cross, with fluttering pennons and prancing steeds. The *predella* hung just below, contains four subjects—"Christ in Gethsemane," "The Last Supper," "The Betrayal," and "The Flagellation." Unfortunately, both pictures are so badly lighted that it is almost impossible except on a very bright day to appreciate the colour. The scenes in this *predella* are nearly the same as in that of the Florence Academy, which hangs as part of the altar-piece, No. 164, although it does not seem really to have belonged to it. The two *predelle* must certainly have been painted within a very short time of one another. In both the composition of "The Last Supper" is precisely the same, as well as "The Flagellation." In the "Betrayal" there is the same violent crowd with spears and pennons, surging round the Christ. In the Florence picture, however, there are only three divisions, "The Betrayal" and "The Way to Calvary" forming the background to "The Agony in the Garden," where Christ kneels before a little brook, with the Apostles sleeping in rows behind Him. The broad impressionistic manner in which [Pg 89] they are painted is the same; and, coarse as is the brushwork, dark and heavy as is the colour, especially in the flesh tints, they are yet exceedingly fine examples of Signorelli's bold style and quick resolute workmanship, and well illustrate his power of rendering violent combined movement, in the crowds which throng round the betrayed Christ, and march tumultuously on the way to Calvary.

The "Madonna and Saints" above this last *predella* (No. 164) although according to Signor Milanesi, not its altar-piece, [69] must certainly have been painted somewhere about the same time, for the broad style, tending rather to coarseness, of the work of this period is very noticeable. It was executed for the church of Santa Trinità in Cortona, and Milanesi suggests that it might be the altar-piece ordered in 1521 by the authorities of that church, [70] but the description given by the document of commission is very different, and the picture itself seems to bear evidence of an earlier date. Like so many of the works in this Gallery, the painting has been so thickly daubed over by modern restorers, that it is next to impossible to form a just idea of the original colour; in its present state it is disagreeably crude and heavy, and in any case the overcrowding of the composition would prevent its being considered a successful example of the master's work, although it has his usual stately dignity and impressive qualities in the individual figures. The Virgin sits with the Child on her knee, clad in red robes, over which is [Pg 90] a garment, now smeared over with black paint, but which formerly was covered with gold embroideries. Over her head is a Trinity, in a *mandorla* surrounded by cherubs. On the left stands the Archangel Michael, in Roman armour, holding the balances, in which are little nude figures representing the souls of the dead; on the right stands Gabriel with the lily and scroll containing the Message of the Annunciation. Below, seated at the foot of the throne, are Saint Augustine and Saint Anastasio, the latter the same burly Bishop with wide-spread knees of the

Loreto Cupola, and the Volterra altarpiece. These two Saints are fine, stately figures, painted with broad sweeping lines. The green robe of S. Anastasio was originally covered with a gorgeous pattern, probably of yellow or gold, but this has been effaced by the thick smear of repaint. The gentle humility in the face of the Virgin recalls the "Madonna," of the Brera Gallery, Milan (No. 197 *bis*) with which the picture has, besides, much in common, the Child, as well as the hands of the Virgin, being exactly the same, although in a reversed position. We shall not probably be far wrong in placing the Florence altar-piece about the same time as this "Madonna," of the Brera, which is dated 1508, and was painted for the church of S. Francesco in Arcevia (a town famous for its possession of one of Signorelli's most important works, which we shall presently consider). Very much repainted, the Madonna still retains great charm and beauty, but the composition is geometrical, and the figures of the Saints uninteresting and empty. In these, especially the standing figure on the left, I feel [Pg 91] the hand of an assistant. With all Signorelli's mannerisms, it lacks his resolute touch and powerful presentation. It is probable that the great inequalities in many of his paintings, especially at this later time, are due to his leaving much of the execution to assistants. Whatever faults are in the work of the master himself, he is never, up to the last, guilty of any feebleness or insipidity, such, for instance, as in the painting of this unsolid figure.

[*Brera, Milan*
MADONNA AND SAINTS
I have been led from one picture to another by reason of similarities of form, and have omitted to speak of a beautiful and important painting, evidently executed soon after the Orvieto frescoes, with which it has much in common. This is the altar-piece in the church of S. Niccolò, Cortona, on one side of which is a "Madonna and Saints," on the other a "Dead Christ upheld by Angels." It is as far as I know, original in idea—this dead Christ supported by the Archangel,

while others show the symbols of the Passion to the group of kneeling Saints. The four Angels are very noble figures, and resemble those of the "Hell" and "Resurrection," of Orvieto. The "S. Jerome" is sincerely painted, and without any of the senile sentimentality with which Signorelli occasionally represents this Saint. The one false note in the work is the stunted figure of the dead Christ, which seems all the more insignificant by contrast with the grand Archangel who supports it. This poetic figure with its great wings and its tender beauty is perhaps the greatest of all the master's renderings of the "Divine Birds." The colour scheme is much lighter than usual, the flesh-tints being especially fair, and the painting [Pg 92] is another instance of those seeming efforts to adopt a less heavy palette, to which I have drawn attention in speaking of the Uffizi *Tondo*.

[*S. Niccolò, Cortona*
DEAD CHRIST UPHELD BY ANGELS
Vischer considers the "Madonna and Saints" on the reverse of the panel to have been painted at a different date. [71] It is an exceedingly fine picture, with all the great qualities of majestic beauty. The Virgin sits enthroned between SS. Peter and Paul, robed in red, and wearing a blue mantle lined with green. The Child, half lying on her knee, has his hand raised in act to bless. It is well modelled, and of a more pleasing type than usual.

In 1507 was painted another very important work—the altar-piece in the church of S. Medardo in Arcevia, a splendid *Ancona*, still in its original Gothic frame. The Virgin is of the same tender type as in the Brera and Florence Academy pictures, but with an added stateliness and gravity. In the centre panel she sits enthroned, with the Child on her knee, clad in an embroidered robe, on the breast of which are two naked cherubs. On the left stand S. Medardo and S. Sebastian, on the right S. Andrew and S. Rock, each figure separated, as in the old polyptychs, by the pilasters of the frame. Above is God the Father, with two Saints on either side, left S. Paul and S. John the Baptist, right S. Peter and S. James of Camerino. Each of the side pilasters of the frame is divided into seven small spaces, each containing the half figure of a saint, the work of assistants. The effect of the whole painting is of great splendour, the colours are of glowing depth, and the richness enhanced by the [Pg 93] low relief in gilded gesso of some of the brocades. But with all its state and dignity, perhaps the most important part of the altar-piece is the *predella* with its five beautiful pictures, flanked on either side by the arms of Arcevia. As colour these are remarkably fine and are treated with more care and less rapidity than Signorelli usually gave to *predella* work, while retaining the same breadth and freedom of general effect. "The Annunciation," with its beautiful perspective, is one of his best compositions of this subject, in which he is always so successful. "The Nativity" recalls that of the Uffizi *predella*; "The Adoration of the Magi" is a fine rendering of the scene, but the two last are the most interesting as well as being the best in workmanship. In "The Flight into Egypt" the painter has evidently been influenced by the engravings of Albrecht Dürer, and has painted the little fortified town of the background very much in his manner. "The Murder of the Innocents" contains two figures in splendid action, the executioners, one with his dagger raised in act to strike, the other holding the child up by the leg—both magnificent studies of the nude, and worthy of the painter of the Orvieto frescoes.

[*In possession of Mr Jarvis, New Haven, U.S.A.*

THE ADORATION OF THE MAGI

Very inferior is the altar-piece of "The Baptism," in the same church of S. Medardo. The existence of the contract of commission, dated June 5, 1508, [72] shows that Signorelli bound himself to paint the [Pg 94] figures of Christ, of the Baptist, and of God the Father, with his own hand, leaving the rest of the work to his best pupils. These figures are, however, so different from any of the master's own work, that it is difficult to believe that they are entirely by him. The picture had evidently to be finished in great haste, since the receipt for payment in Luca's hand is dated the 24th of the same month of June, thus leaving only nineteen days between commission and completion, a very short time for so large a work. The Baptist stands in a rich red mantle pouring the water on the head of the Herculean Christ, who wears the Pollaiuolesque striped loin-cloth. The coarseness and exaggeration of the muscular development have not the characteristics of Signorelli's own errors in over-realism, but bear the same relation to his style that the work of Bandinelli bears to that of Michelangelo. Above is a feeble figure of God the Father, and in the middle distance a man pulls off his shirt, reminding one, both in form and treatment, of the figures in Pier dei Franceschi's "Baptism," of the National Gallery. Another sits by the river putting on a sandal, not unlike, although very inferior to, the athlete of the Munich *Tondo*. The composition is grand, and in the importance given by it to the two principal figures we certainly see the work of Signorelli. The picture is an example of one of those mysterious conflicts of documentary and internal evidence, which the study of Art occasionally furnishes. It still remains in its beautiful original frame, in the gables of which is painted an "Annunciation," and below, on each side, three half figures of Saints by some assistant, who was [Pg 95] not even a pupil of Signorelli, but obviously a follower of Niccolò da Foligno. The *predella* contains five scenes. "The Birth of the Baptist," "The Preaching in the Desert," "The Denouncing of Herod and Herodias" (a *Tondo*), "The Feast of Herod," and—rather out of its due course, since the head is offered in the charger in the fourth scene—"The Decapitation in Prison."

There is a very beautiful fragment of an unknown *predella* in the possession of Mr Jarvis of New Haven, U.S.A., which belongs approximately to this period. It has all the impressive dignity and breadth of treatment of Signorelli's best work. The subject is conceived with special feeling for its stateliness, Joseph standing by the side of the Virgin to receive the gifts, as a Chamberlain might stand beside the throne, while the earnest reverence of the kneeling King, who has cast his crown at the feet of the Child, is most nobly rendered. The gold in the brocaded robes is here slightly in relief. The face of the kneeling King recalls that of the aged Apostle in "The Institution of the Eucharist," Cortona, a painting dated 1512; a beautiful picture, executed for the high altar of the Gesù, but which has now been removed to the Cathedral. Like the other works in this choir it is very badly lighted, and the photograph is also indistinct. Vasari writes of it: "In the Compagnia del Gesù, in the same city (Cortona), he painted three pictures, of which the one over the high altar is marvellous, where Christ communicates the Apostles, and Judas puts the wafer in his satchel." [73] At the end of a shallow hall, in the usual [Pg 96] good perspective, His head accentuated against the sky, as in Leonardo's "Last Supper," Christ stands, and puts the sacred wafer in the mouth of a kneeling Apostle. In the foreground Judas, with a crafty look, opens his satchel. The composition is exceedingly fine, the twelve Apostles making a stately frame for the central figure of Christ. The attitudes and gestures are natural and dramatic, and the faces have individual character.

The two other pictures of which Vasari speaks as having also been painted for the Gesù, now the Baptistery, are—"The Nativity" (a coarse and badly-painted school picture, having affinities with that of the National Gallery, London, No. 1133), and a "Madonna and Saints," which still remains in the Baptistery. Here the Virgin sits, with a Bishop on either side, and two monks below. Dry and precise in composition, like that of the Brera, and apparently painted with the assistance of pupils, the Madonna herself is still very characteristic of the master, and not unlike those of the Brera and the Florence Academy. The picture is in an exceedingly ruined state, and the gabled top in which is painted God the Father, though not without merit, does not belong to the original painting, but is of a later date.

Lastly, we may place in this group, the broadly-painted *predella*, which hangs now, badly lighted, in the sacristy of the Arezzo Cathedral. It is unknown to what altar-piece it belonged, and the pictures are now divided and separately framed. The first represents "The Birth of the Virgin," the second "The Presentation," and the last "The Marriage." "The Presentation" is the finest in composition and general effect, and [Pg 97] contains very stately figures of Joachim and Anna, with splendidly draped robes, and behind them a fine austere landscape. All three pictures are broadly painted and swept in in the usual impressionistic manner.

FOOTNOTES:

[67] Vasari, iii. 686.
[68] See p. 10.
[69] Vasari, iii. 70. Commentario.
[70] See Chronological Table, p. 127.

[71] Vischer, p. 259.
[72] For these notices see Anselmi's monograph, "A proposito della classificazione dei monumenti nazionali nella provincia d'Ancona." (Foligno, 1888), p. 35. Also quoted by Cavalcaselle e Crowe, viii. p. 480.
[73] Vasari, iii, 686.
[Pg 98]

CHAPTER VII

LAST WORKS

We have now considered in detail most of the important works of Signorelli's early manhood and maturity, and up to his seventy-fourth year have found him, both in conception and execution, still maintaining a high standard of excellence, and at an age when the life's work is supposed to be over showing but little sign of failing powers. On the contrary, he seems to have gained ground in certain things most characteristic of his technical ability—in a rugged strength of modelling, in facility of drawing and freedom of brushwork, and particularly in that mastery of united movement, which it seemed his special desire to attain. Even in this last group of paintings which we have now to consider the mind works as powerfully, and the subjects are conceived with the same impressive grandeur, as before, and only in one or two instances can it be noticed that the hand does not always respond so readily to the purpose.

In the "Madonna and Saints," of the Mancini collection, Città di Castello, a slight technical falling off is apparent, although it is possible that this may be due to the assistance of pupils. Its history would seem, however, to point to its being the unaided work of Signorelli; but, as we have already seen, documentary [Pg 99] evidence is by no means infallible. In the archives of Montone, a little town near Umbertide, a deed, dated September 10, 1515, was discovered, which speaks of an altar-piece presented by the master as a free gift to a certain French physician, Luigi de Rutanis, in gratitude "for services rendered, and for those which he hoped to receive in future." [74]

[Mancini Coll., Città di Castello
MADONNA AND SAINTS

The Virgin stands heavily on the heads of cherubs, with S. Sebastian on one side, and Santa Cristina, with a terribly realistic millstone hung round her neck, on the other. Two angels hold the crown over her head, and below stand S. Jerome and S. Nicholas of Bari, both intently reading. The background stretches away into a charming distant landscape, in which is a lake, not unlike Trasimeno, and sloping hills, on which scenes of pastoral life are taking place. This landscape, taken by itself, is the best part of the painting; of the rest, the composition is too mechanically precise, the values of distance are bad, the figures being all on the same plane, and even the landscape does not keep its proper place in the picture. This last fault may, however, be due to repainting, which is so thick that it is useless to speak of the present colour. The altarpiece was discovered by Signor Giacomo Mancini in a cellar in Montone, almost destroyed by damp and neglect, and since its restoration it is perhaps hardly fair to discuss more than the general lines; yet these, in the awkwardness of arrangement, and the comparative triviality of the figures, both in attitude and gesture, betray a weakness we have not hitherto met with. [Pg 100]

Another picture of the same date—1515—is "The Madonna and Saints," in the church of San Domenico, Cortona, also in very bad condition. The restoration of the seventeenth century added a piece of canvas all round, in order to enlarge it. It was painted for Serninio, Bishop of Cortona, whose portrait is to be seen in the corner, full of expression and exceedingly well modelled. The Virgin, in red robe and green mantle, sits with her feet resting on the heads of cherubs, with an angel on either side, and below S. Peter Martyr, and S. Domenico. It is an important work, and among the most successful of the later paintings, and it is curious that it should not have been photographed by either of the larger firms.

The next year, 1516, Signorelli painted "The Deposition," of Umbertide, in which he shows all the technical power of his maturity—(or was it, perhaps, that he left less of the execution to assistants?). It was executed for the little dark church of Santa Croce, in this village, till recently called La Fratta, and still stands over the high altar—not, however, in its original frame, which was removed in the seventeenth century. It seems that there was a lunette over the top, containing a Pietà. [75] Terribly defaced by bad restoration, and the cracking of the later paint, it is still a very beautiful work, and its *predella* has all the qualities of boldness and freedom characteristic of the master's best times. Some of the figures are perhaps too obviously life-studies, especially the Mary, standing in the foreground left, which he evidently painted straight from some *contadina*, whose stolid features he reproduced [Pg 101] without reference to the subject. The body of the Christ is successful, and has all the weight and helpless inertia of a corpse;

the composition is admirable, and there is sincerity of emotion in the painting of much of the scene. It is, however, in the three pictures of the *predella* that we shall find most proof of the vigour of mind and hand. It is interesting to compare Signorelli's treatment of the same subject with that of Pier dei Franceschi in Arezzo, at the painting of which he probably assisted, more than forty years before—"The March of Constantine," "The Discovery of the Cross," and "The Entry of Heraclius into Jerusalem." The first of the three is the best, both for the special quality of animated movement, and for the excellence of its composition and its effect of spacious movement. How much larger a tiny panel like this appears than some of the crowded altar-pieces of his later years! Dashed in with a few broad touches, as a modern impressionist might paint, the scene of the camp is most natural, with its groups of soldiers and marching troops with raised lances and fluttering pennons.

true one in the resuscitation of the dead youth. In the third—"The Entry of Heraclius into Jerusalem"—we have again a splendid effect of a moving body of men. The Emperor has descended from his horse, which is led [Pg 102] behind him, and barefooted, in his shirt, he carries the Cross within the gates.

The next dated work—"The Madonna and Saints," of the Arezzo Gallery, was painted three years after this, in 1519. "He executed," says Vasari, "in his old age, a picture for the Compagnia of S. Girolamo, part of which was paid for by Messer Niccolò Gamurrini, Doctor of Law, Master of the Rolls, whom he portrayed from life in that picture, on his knees before the Madonna, to whom he is presented by a S. Nicholas, also in the said picture; there are besides, S. Donato and S. Stephen, and below a nude S. Jerome, and a David who sings on a Psaltery; there are also two Prophets, who appear, by the scrolls in their hands, to be discussing the Conception." [76]

In this picture it is in the intention rather than the execution that we shall find the vigour and strength which ended only with the painter's life. Much still remains grand and impressive, but though it shows considerable power, the actual work is not so good. The colour is exceedingly dark, and full of harsh contrasts; the composition is overcrowded, as in many of his later paintings; and the figure of David, although nobly conceived, is awkward and ill-balanced. On the other hand, the Virgin is as powerfully executed as ever, and so is the earnest, white-haired Prophet at her feet. It seems to me that the master has given [Pg 103] his own features in this upturned face, with its firmly-cut lips and square jaw, certainly much more real a person than the apathetic kneeling Donor. After its removal from its original place over the altar of the Confraternity, the picture was for several years in Santa Croce, and, after the suppression of that convent in 1849, removed to Santo Spirito, and from thence to the Gallery.

Very close to it in style, and probably painted at no distant date, is the *predella* owned by Mr Ludwig Mond. It has three stories—I. Ahasuerus and Esther, II. and III. (with no legendary connection of which I am aware) Scenes in the Life of S. Augustine. The first is the finest. Ahasuerus, surrounded by his councillors, bends forward, and touches with his sceptre the head of the kneeling Esther. His figure is very like that of the David in the foregoing picture. On the right is a fine back view of one of the characteristic swaggering soldiers in tight striped clothes. The treatment is broad, but the drawing in parts is somewhat careless. In the other two scenes, the composition is jerky and insignificant, but the individual figures are characteristic, especially the nude *écorché*-like old saint. They represent visions which appear in the air to S. Augustine, who sits below under a *loggia*.

Again, very close to the Arezzo altar-piece is "The Conception of the Virgin," painted for the church of the Gesù, Cortona, now in the Cathedral. The Virgin stands, on the usual cherub heads, in red

[*Santa Croce, Umbertide*]
THE DEPOSITION

[*Gallery, Arezzo*]
MADONNA, SAINTS, AND PROPHETS

The commission was given to Luca by the Compagnia of S. Girolamo, on September 19, 1519, and the price was to be one hundred broad gold florins, to be shared by Messer Gamurrini and the Confraternity.

and blue robes, while God the Father bends over her, and two angels scatter flowers through the air. Below are six [Pg 104] prophets, among them David, with his Psaltery, and Solomon, in crown and royal robe. Under the Virgin, apparently supporting the cherubs, is the Tree of Life, with two very fine nude figures of Adam and Eve receiving the fruit from the serpent. It is the lower part only we have to consider, the whole of the upper painting, with the weak, badly-draped Virgin and the theatrical angels being certainly the work of assistants, as also, it seems to me, is the drapery of the half-kneeling Prophet to the right. The David is exactly the same figure as in the Arezzo altar-piece, to which, besides, there is a great resemblance in all the faces, and in the hard coarse manner in which the draperies are treated. The picture, however, lacks the rugged strength which makes the Arezzo picture, with all its shortcomings, so impressive, and only in the nude figures is the old power unimpaired. These, however, are very good, the Adam especially being as fine a study of the human form as any of the earlier work.

At Morra, a little village not far from Città di Castello, in the church of San Crescenziano, are two very important frescoes, a "Crucifixion" and a "Flagellation," evidently very late work of the master. In the latter the composition is very little altered from the early picture of the Brera. Christ is in the centre, bound to the pillar, and on the right stands the Roman soldier. The executioner near him is almost a repetition of the magnificent drawing in the Louvre (see reproduction), except that the legs are wide apart. All Signorelli's energies have again gone into the figures of the executioners, but, fine as they [Pg 105] are, they are not treated with the same breadth as in the earlier picture, albeit the painting is free almost to roughness. The background, instead of the carved wall, now opens out of the court into a spacious landscape.

In the "Crucifixion," the group at the foot of the Cross is arranged much like those of the San Sepolcro, Urbino, and Cortona pictures, but it is half lost in the confusion of a crowd of mounted soldiers. The impressive silence and solemnity of these earlier "Pietàs" is changed here to a scene of noisy turmoil, and the painter's interest is obviously centred on the movement of this hustling crowd. The horses are badly drawn and ill-balanced, as in the Louvre "Adoration," and the Magdalen is very coarsely painted. The animation and action are well rendered, but something of the grandeur of his earlier work is sacrificed.

This grandeur was, however, fully regained in the last work of the master, painted in 1523, the very year of his death—"The Coronation of the Virgin," in the Collegiata of Foiano, a small town near Sinalunga.

The Virgin, in red robes and greenish-blue mantle, with fair hair, kneels before Christ, who places the crown on her head. On either side two angels play musical instruments, and on the right and left stand S. Joseph and the Archangel Michael. In the foreground kneels S. Martin, to whom the altar-piece was dedicated, in a magnificent gold cope, having on his left S. Jerome with a grey loin-cloth. Farther back are three monks, and behind S. Martin stands the Magdalen, while on the other side an old saint introduces the donor, Angelo Massarelli. The general tone of colour is not nearly so heavy as in the [Pg 106] Arezzo painting, the reds are of a pale rose-colour, and only the flesh-tints of S. Jerome are very dark. This figure and the S. Martin are nobly and powerfully conceived. The donor recalls the portrait of the Gamurrini of Arezzo.

The painting does not seem to be the unassisted work of Signorelli, the S. Michael being too insignificant a figure, and the Magdalen too weakly executed to be by his own hand. The *predella* bears evidence that he had an assistant, for, of the four stories of S. Martin, which they illustrate, only two are by the master. These two are very fine and bold, in composition and brushwork. In the first the Saint, clad in armour, is seated on the characteristic white horse, with a man-at-arms behind him, and divides his cloak with the nude beggar. The background is a broadly-painted landscape. The other represents the Saint kneeling before a Bishop and two acolytes, clothed in a green tabard, a romantic and beautiful figure. The two remaining divisions are larger in size, and obviously the work of assistants, one illustrating S. Martin exorcising a mad bull, the other his funeral and the miraculous healing of the sick by the dead body.

It is satisfactory to have to conclude the list of works with one so strong, and which combines so many of the qualities which we have learnt to look for in Signorelli's painting. Rugged energy, dignity, decorative grace, and even romantic beauty are all to be found in this altar-piece, which is a fit ending to the life's work of the master. [77]

FOOTNOTES:

[74] Transcribed in Vischer, p. 360.
[75] Cavalcaselle e Crowe, viii. 493.
[76] Vasari, iii. 692.
[77] These detailed studies do not include all the works of Signorelli, but a complete list of all that are known to the author is to be found in the catalogue at the end.
[Pg 107]

CHAPTER VIII

DRAWINGS

The study of Signorelli's drawings is unsatisfactory, both by reason of their scarcity, and the enormous difference of merit, even among those few which can be considered as genuine. Morelli writes: "His drawings are found in all the most important collections of Europe," [78] but he mentions only thirteen, and although many certainly in all the galleries bear his name, and the impress of his influence, later study appears to accept only six as by his own hand; and of these six two are so much inferior to the rest that I cannot bring myself to feel any degree of certainty as to their genuineness.

This difficulty of acceptance arises from a comparison with the very high standard of excellence in the two magnificent studies of the nude in the Louvre collection, which correspond, in breadth of feeling, in grandeur of pose, and in boldness and accuracy of touch, to his best brushwork.

No. 345, formerly in the Baldinucci collection, represents two nude male figures of superb proportions, one standing with his hands on his hips, the other, in the characteristic attitude with wide-spread, firmly-planted feet, having his hand on the shoulder of the [Pg 108] first. It is in black chalk, dashed in swiftly, with bold sweeping strokes, apparently direct from the life. It is one of the finest studies of the nude in existence, both for the splendid anatomy of the figures and the freedom and energy of touch. No. 343, also from the Baldinucci collection, which is here reproduced, is hardly inferior to it in the same qualities of boldness and freedom. It seems to be the study from which Signorelli painted the executioner in *grisaille* near the "Pietà," in Orvieto, and later the scourging figure of the Morra "Flagellation," although in both there are slight differences of position. The action is exceedingly fine, the poise of the figure on the well-drawn feet being especially good, while all the force of the strong body is thrown into the arms stretched high up over the head.

In Dresden is a sheet of studies, which, while less fine than these two, are yet very characteristic, and undoubtedly genuine. They are also in black chalk, but very much rubbed, and consequently rather indistinct They represent four nude figures in different postures, which Morelli considers to be studies for part of the Orvieto frescoes, although I have failed to discover there anything which corresponds to them.

[*Louvre, Paris*
STUDY OF NUDE FIGURE
In the Uffizi Gallery, Florence, is another black chalk study of two men being chained by devils, which, again, seems as though it must have been intended for some of the figures in the "Damnation," but which I cannot find there. This drawing is also very characteristic, and although falling far below the merit of

the Louvre studies, has all Signorelli's qualities of dramatic energy and strength of touch. [Pg 109]

The heavy, coarse study for a "Death of Lucretia," also in the Uffizi, I find extremely hard, in comparison with any of the foregoing, to accept as an undoubted work of the master, although I am not prepared to absolutely deny it. There is a want of proportion in the figures, and an indecision in the strokes, hard to reconcile with all we know of his work.

In the collection at Windsor is another chalk drawing—"Hercules overcoming Antæus"—of little merit either of anatomy or of technique, but which may possibly be from his hand. There is something of the influence of Antonio Pollaiuolo visible in this treatment of his favourite subject, and it is just conceivable that it may be an early study by Signorelli done in his workshop.

The list of all the drawings which are attributed to him in different collections would take too long for the slight purpose it would serve; but for the benefit of those who desire to compare for themselves those which Morelli and Vischer decide to be genuine, I have added a list of their attributions, transcribed without addition or correction.

DRAWINGS MENTIONED BY MORELLI
Dresden (*Gallery*).—Study of four nude figures.
Florence (*Uffizi*).—Case 459. [No. 1246.]
London (*Brit. Mus.*).—Three drawings, in vol. 32.
Paris (*Louvre*).—[Nos. 340, 341, 342, 343, 344, 345, 346.]
Windsor (*Library*).—A drawing, attributed to Masaccio. [Pg 110]

Besides these, a design for Marcantonio's engraving of "Mars, Venus, and Cupid" (Bartsch, 345), attributed to Mantegna.

DRAWINGS FROM VISCHER'S LIST OF SIGNORELLI'S WORKS
Berlin (*Gallery*).—Man's head with cap (exposed in frame).
Chatsworth. —Four Saints (Waagen's attribution).
Dresden (*Gallery*) Case I. 10.—Head of a Woman. (Exposed in room II.).—Battlefield (?) [This so-called Battlefield is the study of four nudes, mentioned among the genuine drawings.—*Author's Note.*]
Florence (*Uffizi*).—Figure of Youth. Two Damned bound by Devils. Nude Figure bearing Corpse. Madonna and Child (doubtful). Death of Lucretia (?). Bacchanal.
Paris (*Louvre*) 340.—Four nude figures; black chalk. 341. Two Saints; coloured chalk. 342. A Saint; coloured chalk. 343. Nude figure scourging; black chalk. 344. A Saint; black chalk. 345. Two nude figures. 346. Pietà. 347. Nude figure bearing corpse; water-colour (more finished repetition of the Uffizi study).
Siena (*Collection of Mr C. Fairfax Murray*).—Seated Saints (study for *grisaille* Prophets in the nave of the church of Loreto).
Windsor (*Collection of H.M. the Queen*).—Devil seizing man; black chalk (study for Orvieto frescoes). Male figure in three positions; Indian ink (attributed to Raffael).

[*Academy, Florence*
MAGDALEN AT THE FOOT OF THE CROSS

FOOTNOTES:
[78] "Italian Painters," i. 93.

[Pg 111]

CHAPTER IX

PUPILS AND GENERAL INFLUENCE

It would not be possible, in the space at my disposal, to go with any thoroughness into the work of Signorelli's imitators, even of those who fell directly under his influence. The painters who stand foremost among them, Don Bartolommeo della Gatta and Girolamo Genga, are both too important to be dealt with in a short notice, while it would be a thankless as well as an arduous task, to try to distinguish the different painters of what is generically classed as school-work, being, as it nearly always is, without either individuality or merit. I shall do little more, therefore, than make a brief mention of the names and principal works of the known imitators, and try instead to indicate the influence of Signorelli's style upon painting in general.

Morelli says much of his "uncompromising guidance," and of the "degeneration" of those who fell under his "crushing influence." [79] Something of the sort has been said of Michelangelo, and might be said of every strong man whose personality is powerful enough to stamp its mark on his contemporaries, but since no one who is content to be merely a copyist could produce valuable work, the world has probably lost little by the submission. It is, however, true that, [Pg 112] as the powerful muscles of Michelangelo's statues become meaningless lumps in the works of Bandinelli and Vasari, so the mannerisms of Signorelli, which were the outward sign of his strong and energetic temperament, lost all significance, and were merely coarse exaggerations in the work of his imitators. The swaggering attitude, the freedom of gesture, and the dramatic expression, shorn of the strength and earnest emotion from which they sprang, became disagreeably incongruous in the pictures of the feeble painters who imitated them.

But one, at least, of Signorelli's disciples was neither slavish nor feeble. Bartolommeo della Gatta, otherwise Piero di Antonio Dei, the most important of those who came under his influence, was a painter of great charm and ability. If it be true, as a recent criticism has pronounced, that the beautiful "Madonna," of the Christ Church collection, Oxford, there attributed to Pier dei Franceschi, is from his brush, [80] we have to deal with a man who started work under the same ennobling influence as Signorelli himself. Be that as it may, and as future research will decide, the fresco of "The Death of Moses," in the Sistine Chapel, which later study has presumed to be almost entirely his work, proves him to be a painter of great beauty and importance. Signor Gaetano Milanesi has thrown doubt upon his existence as a painter of anything except miniatures, [81] but the happy discovery of a document, referring to his altar-piece of "S. Francis receiving the stigmata," in the Church of that Saint in Castiglione Fiorentino, has [Pg 113] placed the fact beyond dispute. [82] The student who desires to know more of this painter is referred to the last Italian edition of Cavalcaselle e Crowe, vol. viii., and to the "Life" by Vasari, whose reliability in this case the researches of the critics so well confirm. Born probably in 1408, he was already a man of mature age when Signorelli himself was a child, but his simple, pliable nature fitted him to be a follower rather than a leader, and we find him now influenced by Pier dei Franceschi, now by Signorelli, and again later by Fiorenzo di Lorenzo. If it be true that the really splendid painting of the Sistine Chapel is due to him entirely, it is, of course, his masterpiece, and reaches, indeed, a level not very inferior to that of Signorelli himself. His most important undisputed works are the abovementioned painting in the church of S. Francesco, Castiglione Fiorentino, the altar-piece in the Collegiata of the same town, a S. Rock in the Gallery, and a fresco of S. Jerome, in the Bishop's Palace, Arezzo, etc.

Another imitator of importance, Girolamo Genga, impressionable as his nature was, yet has much individual excellence to distinguish him from the rest of Signorelli's assistants. Born at Urbino in 1476, he was placed, at the age of fifteen, in the studio of Signorelli, with whom, according to Vasari, he remained for twenty years, becoming "one of the best pupils that he had." [83] After assisting the master in the painting of the Cappella Nuova, Orvieto, Genga (always according to the same authority) placed himself to study perspective with [Pg 114] Perugino, at the time that Raffaelle was also under the influence of that painter. This, as well as the fact that he was a native of Urbino, and had probably also felt the impression of Timoteo Viti, would account for the enormous influence Raffaelle's painting had upon his later work. He seems to have had an extraordinary facility for changing his style; for, while under the influence of Signorelli, as in the Petrucci Palace frescoes (Nos. 375 and 376 in the Gallery of Siena), his work bears so much resemblance to that of the master, that so observant a critic as Morelli declared the composition of both to be most certainly by Luca himself. [84] Genga seems to have caught, not the superficial forms only, but also the spirit of Signorelli in these frescoes, for in one—"The Flight of Æneas from Troy"—there is an exaggeration of the characteristic energy and movement, which, almost hysterical though it be, is yet successful and full of real life; while in the swaggering strength of the nude figures in "The Rescue of Prisoners" there is something of Luca's own dignity and impressiveness. In his later work, although he never departs from certain likenesses to his first master, yet he gives himself up to the influence of Raffaelle unreservedly, as may be best seen in the Cesena altar-piece, now in the Brera, Milan. Morelli writes of him: "This eclectic painter, who, though working in a baroque style, is not without talent, is confounded with the most diverse masters, both in drawings and paintings"; [85] and the fact that besides the above-mentioned variations of style, his work is also pardonably attributed [Pg 115] to Girolamo del Pacchia [86] and to Sodoma, [87] fully justifies the epithet and the assertion. Of the other and less important followers, Tommaso Bernabei, called Papacello, seems to have been first assistant of Giulio Romano, and then of Giambattista Caporali, with whom he is said to have painted the frescoes in the Villa Passerini, near Cortona. His first original work is of the year 1524—a "Conception of the Virgin," in the church of Santa Maria del Calcinaio, near Cortona, in which the manner of Signorelli is very apparent. In the same church are two other paintings by him, dated 1527, an "Adoration of the Magi," and an "Annunciation," which are sufficient to indicate the small amount of artistic ability of the painter. The date of his birth is unknown; he died in 1559. [88]

We have, besides, four members of Signorelli's own family. First, his son Polidoro, whom we know to have been his assistant at Orvieto; for, in a document of 1501, he is mentioned as having received certain payments there for salary, as well as for materials for the work. [89] His manner of painting is unknown to us, so that it is impossible to distinguish his share in the frescoes.

Two other sons, Antonio and Pier Tommaso, were, it seems, also assistants of their father, the former being the painter of a dated altar-piece in the church of Santa Maria del Calcinaio, near Cortona. [90] Lastly, his nephew Francesco, the most important of the assistants bearing [Pg 116] his own name, from whose hand there are several paintings very close to the master in style. To him, at least, are attributed the standard of "The Baptism," in the Gallery of Città di Castello, and a *Tondo* of a "Madonna and Saints," in the Palazzo Pubblico, Cortona. There is one signed altar-piece by him, "The Conception of the Virgin," in the choir of S. Francesco, Gubbio.

Turpino Zaccagna is another pupil, of whom Manni writes that he was a noble youth of Cortona, who took to painting, and imitated Signorelli's style. [91] Of his work remains an altar-piece in the church of S. Agata di Cantalena, near Cortona, signed and dated 1537.

With him the list of known pupils closes. But more really important than either of these minor scholars is the unknown imitator who painted the beautiful "Magdalen," of the Florence Academy. Executed on linen, and evidently intended for a church standard, this is the most successful of all the works in Signorelli's manner, which yet cannot be accepted as genuine. The design of the principal figures in the foreground and middle distance I believe to be by Signorelli himself, and the intensity of emotion in the Magdalen, who has cast herself at the foot of the Cross, and the impressive grandeur of the three figures to the right, have lost none of the original spirit of the master. The colour is entirely different, and would alone preclude the acceptance of the painting as Signorelli's work, but, moreover, the general effect has so little of his sweeping breadth, and the details of the shadowy landscape are so [Pg 117] poorly composed, that it is probable even the whole of the drawing is not by him.

[*Gallery, Buda-Pesth*
TIBERIUS GRACCHUS

An interesting picture in the Gallery of Buda-Pesth, there attributed to Luca himself, connects the charming and mysterious "Griselda" series (Nos. 912, 913, and 914), of the National Gallery, [92] with some follower of Signorelli, for it is sufficient to glance at

the background of this "Tiberius Gracchus" to be convinced that its painter is the same unknown master. In the "Griselda" pictures there is more evidence than here of the influence of Pintorricchio, to whom they are, not unnaturally, attributed; while in the "Tiberius," in the drapery of the figure, and the type of the children who support the tablet, especially, there is much of the real spirit of Signorelli, as well as a good deal of his breadth and solidity of drawing. The painter must, for the present, remain as an unknown Umbrian, almost equally influenced by Pintorricchio and Luca, and with peculiar qualities of simple grace and romance, which give his work an extremely individual character.

Very different is the imitation of Signorelli's mannerisms in such works as "The Nativity," of the National Gallery, "The Madonna and Saints," of the Gallery of Città di Castello, and "The Abbondanza," of the Uffizi. In these the imitation is mechanical, and without any comprehension of the master's spirit. It would be useless to mention more of the school-work, in which superficial excellences and defects are copied with equal zeal. [Pg 118]

On the other hand, the spiritual qualities which these mechanical imitators missed, were felt intensely by men who never adopted his mannerisms, and it is in the work of these that the real effect of Signorelli's influence is to be found. The frescoes of Orvieto never became, like Masaccio's in the Carmine, a school to which the younger painters thronged, purposely to learn the methods of the master, but their impressive grandeur and solemnity, and the breadth of brushwork and solid modelling by which these qualities were in a great measure obtained, worked, nevertheless, a very important change in the Art of the time, and a wave of strong fresh blood was sent through its veins. Without them, perhaps, we should never have had the same appeal to the imagination and the nobler instincts in the Sistine paintings, although there is not in the whole of the work one single mannerism from Signorelli's style.

[93] But what is called the "Terribilità" of the older master was entirely free from the sombre melancholy which strikes so gloomy a note in the work of Michelangelo. Signorelli's greatest gift to us is his conception of humanity, not only of its robust strength, but of its mental vigour. His figures are solemn, but it is a solemnity untainted with sadness, conscious only of the dignity of the human race, its significance and responsibilities.

By his power over his materials, won by hard study, he added much to Art, and presented things, not as conventional symbols, but as they are actually reflected [Pg 119] on the eye. His people stand on solid ground by the help of firm muscle, substantial realities that we feel could be touched and walked round. His atmosphere gives the sense of real space and air. His trees seem to have roots, and their branches to be full of sap. By this truth and power of presenting things as they are he was able to endow his paintings with his own conception of Nature, grander and wider than our own, and to make us see mankind with his eyes, built on broader, stronger lines. Nothing trivial or insignificant enters into his perception of life. He takes his place with Mantegna, with Dürer, and with Cossa, the austere painters, who felt the dignity of life to lie in rugged strength, iron resolution, and unflinching self-reliance.

FOOTNOTES:

[79] "Italian Painters," i. 96.
[80] An attribution of Mr B. Berensen.
[81] See "Commentary on the Life of Bart. della Gatta." Vasari, iii. 227.
[82] Cavalcaselle e Crowe. Transcript of the Document, viii. 537.
[83] Vasari, vi. 315.
[84] "Italian Painters," i. 94.
[85] "Italian Painters," ii. 285.
[86] Madonna. Siena Gallery, No. 340.
[87] Portrait of Man. Pitti Gallery, Florence, No. 382.
[88] See Cavalcaselle e Crowe, viii. 521.
[89] Vischer, 102.
[90] Vischer, 320.
[91] Inserted at the end of Vischer's "Signorelli," 383.
[92] Unfortunately recently hung so high that any just appreciation of their great merit and beauty is impossible.
[93] Crowe and Cavalcaselle maintain that Raffaelle also studied carefully the works of Signorelli. See Cavalcaselle e Crowe, viii. 425, and i. 41, etc. etc.
[Pg 121]

CHRONOLOGICAL TABLE OF THE LIFE AND WORKS OF LUCA SIGNORELLI

[The following table is compiled from that of Cavalcaselle e Crowe. (Le Monnier, 1898) as being more complete than that in Milanesi's Vasari, and more condensed than that of Vischer. Dates, however, which are not supported by documentary evidence have been omitted.]

1441 (*circa*). Luca was born of Egidio, son of Luca, son of Ventura Signorelli.

1474. (November) Completed the fresco in the Tower of the Commune, Città di Castello, with the Virgin enthroned between SS. Jerome and Paul, first spoiled by exposure, and completely destroyed by the earthquake of 1789.

1479. (Sep. 6) Elected to the Consiglio dei XVIII., Cortona.

1479. (Nov. 28) Elected to the Conservatori degli Ordinamente del Comune.

1480. Elected to the Priori for the months of March and April.

1480. (Aug. 26) Elected to the Consiglio Generale.

1481. (Aug. 25) Elected to the Consiglio Generale.

1484. Painted the altar-piece in the Cathedral of Perugia.

1484. Is sent to Gubbio, to negotiate with Francesco di Giorgio, Sienese architect, for a design for the church of Calcinaio, near Cortona.

1485. (Jan. 10) Undertook the painting of a chapel in Sant' Agata, Spoleto; a work which, it seems, was never executed. [Pg 122]

1485. (Feb. 22) Elected to the Consiglio dei XVIII.

1485. (Aug. 22) Elected to the Consiglio Generale.

1486. Elected to the Priori for the months of January and February.

1488. (July 6) For the great ability with which he painted the Banner of the Blessed Virgin, is made citizen of Città di Castello, as was his great desire.

1488. Reseated in the Chief Magistracy of Cortona for the months of September and October.

1489. Elected to the Consiglio Generale.

1490. (Dec. 25) Elected to the Priori for the months of January and February.

1490. (Dec. 27) His son Antonio announces to the Priori that Luca cannot serve, being absent from the city at a distance of over forty miles.

1491. (Jan. 5) Is among those invited to judge the designs and models presented for the competition for the façade of Santa Maria del Fiore, Florence. Did not assist.

1491. (Aug. 23) Elected to the Consiglio Generale.

1491. Painted the altar-piece of the "Annunciation," in the Cathedral, Volterra.

1491. Painted the altar-piece of San Francesco, Volterra.

1493. Painted the altar-piece of the "Adoration of the Magi," for the church of Sant'Agostino, Città di Castello.

1493. Elected to the Consiglio Generale.

1493. (Sept. 24) Sold for 122 gold florins to Domenico di Tommaso della Barba of Cortona, some acres of ground situated in the territory of Montalla, called La Mucchia, and the Via di Montalla, and others in the territory of Orsaia, called the Bocca del Prato and the Via da Loghino.

1494. Commission for the Banner for the church of Santo Spirito, Urbino. [Pg 123]

1495. Elected to the Priori for the months of November and December.

1496. Painted the altar-piece of the "Nativity," for the church of San Francesco, Città di Castello.

1497. Elected to the Priori for the months of May and June.

1497. (March 10) Elected one of the Revisori degli Argenti.

1497. Elected to the Priori for the months of November and December.

1497. Painted in the cloister of Monte Oliveto, near Chiusuri, "Stories in the Life of S. Benedict."

1498. Painted the altar-piece for the chapel of the Bicchi family in S. Agostino, Siena.

1498. (Feb. 22) Elected to the Consiglio Generale.

1499. (April 5) Commission for the frescoes in the roof of the Cappella Nuova, in the Cathedral, Orvieto.

1500. (April 27) Commission for the painting of the walls in the above-mentioned chapel.

1500. (Feb. 21) Elected to the Consiglio Generale.

1501. (May 1) Becomes surety to a citizen who undertakes the office of Priore of the Commune.

1501. Certain payments are made to Polidoro, son of Maestro Luca, for colours and plaster, the removing of the scaffolding of the chapel, and for a part of his salary.

1501. (June 5) Sold to Ventura, his brother, the half of a house, which belonged to him, together with the said Ventura, situated in Cortona, in the quarter of San Marco, bounded by the Hospital of San Niccolò, by Pietro, surnamed Scrolla, by Jacopo di Francesco, and by the Via del Comune.

1502. Painted the "Deposition," for the church of Santa Margherita, Cortona, now in the Cathedral.

1502. Payment made to Maestro Luca Signorelli for the painting of the Cappella Nuova, Orvieto. [Pg 124]

1502. (Feb. 21) Elected to the Consiglio Generale.

1502. (June 23) Elected to the Priori for the months of July and August, but cannot serve because his family is attacked by the plague.

1502. (July 23) Presents to Paolo di Forzore and to his daughter Francesca two acres of ground at Rio di Loreto, belonging to him as heir of his son Antonio, who had received it as the dowry of his first wife Nannina, daughter of Paolo.

1502. Elected to the Priori for the months of November and December. Being absent, his name was removed from the list.

1504. (Feb. 23) Elected to the Council of XVIII.

1504. Elected to the Priori for the months of May and June.

1504. Painted the altar-piece of S. Mary Magdalen for the Cathedral of Orvieto.

1504. (Dec. 5) Payment for the paintings of the Cappella Nuova.

1505. (Feb. 21) Elected to the Consiglio Generale.

1505. (Sept. 1) Is surety for one of the Priori.

1506. Is in Siena, and receives the commission for the cartoon of the "Judgment of Solomon," for the marble pavement of the Cathedral.

1506. (Oct. 27) Is surety for one of the Priori.

1507. (Feb. 20) Elected to the Consiglio Generale.

1507. Elected to the Priori for the months of July and August.

1507. (Dec. 17) Elected to the Council of the Casa di Misericordia.

1507. Painted the altar-piece in the church of S. Medardo, Arcevia.

1508. (Feb. 23) Elected to the Consiglio dei XVIII.

1508. Elected to the Priori for the months of July and August. [Pg 125]

1508. (July 5) Is sent on an embassy to Florence to demand permission to reform the offices and ordinances of the Commune.

1508. (Aug. 25) Elected to the Consiglio Generale.

1508. Is in Rome, painting for Julius II., together with Perugino, Pintorricchio, and Sodoma.

1509. (Feb. 21) Elected one of the Inspectors of Santa Margherita.

1509. (March 1) Becomes surety for a priest.

1509. (March 11) Binds himself to paint, for 70 gold florins, a picture for the high altar of the Convent Church of Santuccie, Cortona.

1509. (Aug. 25) Elected to the Consiglio dei XVIII.

1509. Elected to the Priori for the months of January and February.

1510. (Aug. 18) Appointed one of the Inspectors of Relics of the Cathedral.

1510. Payment for the Cappella Nuova, Orvieto.

1511. (Aug. 28) Elected to the Consiglio Generale.

1511. Elected to the Priori for the months of November and December.

1512. Painted "The Institution of the Eucharist," in the Cathedral, Cortona.

1512. (Sept. 27) Is sent as ambassador to Florence, together with Messer Silvio Passerini, Messer Gilio and Jacopo Vagnucci, to congratulate the Medici on their return to Florence. Departed Sept. 28 and returned Oct. 12.

1513. Is in Rome, and appears to have borrowed money from Michelangelo.

1514. (July 18) Elected to the Riformatori e Imborsatori degli Uffici.

1514. (Aug. 25) Elected to the Sindaco del Capitano.

1514. (March 18) Makes a will, annulling the donation made [Pg 126] to his daughter Gabriella, to his son-in-law Mariotto Passerini, and to his granddaughter Bernardina, and pronouncing as his sole heir his son Pier Tommaso, and his grandson Giulio, son of the above.

1515. (Feb. 18) Elected to the Conservatori degli Ordinamente.

1515. Painted the "Madonna," now in the Mancini collection, Città di Castello.

1515. (Aug. 25) Elected to the Consiglio Generale.

1515. (Sept. 23) Is commissioned by the Priori of Cortona to paint, for 16 gold florins, the arms of Silvio Passerini, Chancellor of Leo X., on the walls of the atrium of the Palazzo Pubblico.

1515-16. Painted the "Deposition," in the church at La Fratta (now Umbertide).

1516. (Feb. 21) Elected to the Collegi.

1516. (Feb. 26) Luca, from the rostrum, speaks publicly in the Council on a matter in deliberation.

1516. (May 21) Elected to the Consiglio Generale; but is absent.

1516. Elected to the Priori for the months of November and December.

1517. (Feb. 22) Among the Stimatori del danno.

1517. (April 23) Among the Inspectors of the Property of Santa Margherita.

1517. (July 24) Is elected as ambassador to Rome to present to Cardinal Passerini a gift from the Commune.

1517. (Aug. 26) Elected to the Consiglio Generale.

1517. (Nov. 9) Is excused from the above-mentioned embassy to Rome.

1518. Elected to the Collegi.

1518. Painted the altar-piece for the Confraternity of San Girolamo of Arezzo.

1520. (Feb. 23) Elected to the Consiglio dei XVIII. [Pg 127]

1520. Elected to the Priori for the months of May and June.

1520. (June 7) Gave the design of a wooden candelabra with copper sconces for the altar of the Great Hall of Council, Cortona.

1520. (Aug. 25) Elected to the Consiglio dei XVIII.

1521. (April 23) Elected Prior of the Confraternity of Sant' Antonio.

1521. (April 27) Commissioned to paint a picture for the Hospital of the Misericordia, Cortona.

1521. (May 22) The Priori writes to Cardinal Passerini, legate to Perugia, that he should not send Maestro Pietro Perugino or other painters to whom Luca may have spoken, to value the picture painted by Luca in the Church of Santa Maria del Pièvé.

1521. (July 7) Commission for the picture for the Convent of S. Trinità in Cortona.

1521. (Aug. 15) Elected to take part in the Commission to examine the new bridge over the Chiana.

1521. (Sept. 6) Elected to the Pacieri.

1522. (Feb. 18) Elected to the Collegi.

1522. (April 23) Prior of the Confraternity of San Marco.

1522. (Aug. 25) Elected one of the Conservatori degli Ordinamente del Comune, and the Provveditori de' luoghi pii.

1522. Elected to the Priori for the months of January and February.

1523. Painted the altar-piece of the Collegiata, Foiano.

1523. (Feb. 21) Elected to the Sindaci del Capitano.

1523. (April 24) Elected one of the Inspectors of the Chapel of Santa Margherita.

1523. (June 14) Received payment for the picture of Foiano.

1523. (June 23) The Priori commission him to paint, for the chapel of the great hall of the Palazzo Pubblico, a picture with "Christ disputing in the Temple," for the price of 35 gold florins. [Pg 128]

1523. (July 16) Elected one of the Riformatori degli Uffici.

1523. (Oct. 13) His last will. Desires to be buried in the church of S. Francesco, in the tomb of his family.

1523. (Oct. 15) Adds a codicil to his will with a few alterations of bequests.

1523. Died between the last days of November and the 1st December. The 8th December another citizen is nominated to the Inspectorship of the Chapel of Santa Margherita, as substitute for Maestro Luca, being dead. [Pg 129]

CATALOGUE OF THE WORKS OF

LUCA SIGNORELLI

ARRANGED ACCORDING TO THE GALLERIES

IN WHICH THEY ARE

CONTAINED.

[Pg 131]

BRITISH ISLES.
DUBLIN, GALLERY.
Feast in the House of Simon. [94]
This must be the panel mentioned by Cavalcaselle as in the possession of Capt. Stirling, Glentyan, Scotland (?).
LIVERPOOL, ROYAL INSTITUTION.
Madonna. Oil. 1 ft. 9 in. × 1 ft. 4 in. [No. 26.]
LONDON, NATIONAL GALLERY.
The Circumcision. Oil. 8 ft. 6 in. × 5 ft. 11 in. [No. 1128.]
Originally in the church of S. Francesco, Volterra. Later in the Duke of Hamilton's Collection, near Glasgow. Purchased in 1882.
Inscribed: LVCAS CORTONENSIS PINXIT.
LONDON, Mr BENSON'S COLLECTION.
Madonna. Two Parts of Predella :
1. Dispute on the way to Emmaus. 2. Christ at Emmaus.
LONDON, LORD CRAWFORD'S COLLECTION.
Two Parts of Predella :
1. Meeting of Joachim and Anna. 2. Birth of the Virgin.
LONDON, Mr LUDWIG MOND'S COLLECTION.
Predella :
1. Ahasuerus and Esther. 2 and 3. Scenes in the Life of S. Augustine. [Pg 132]
LONDON, Mr MUIR MACKENZIE'S COLLECTION.
Madonna. Tondo.
ON SALE IN LONDON.
Annunciation.
Part of Predella formerly in the Mancini Collection, Città di Castello. For sale since 1898.
RICHMOND, COLLECTION OF SIR

FRANCIS COOK.
Two Fragments of a Baptism.
Profile Portrait of Man.
SCOTLAND (COLLECTION OF SIR JOHN STIRLING MAXWELL, POLLOCK HOUSE).
Pietà.

FRANCE.
PARIS, LOUVRE.
Part of Predella. 1525. Oil. 1 ft. 1 in. × 2 ft. 4 in.
From the Collection of Louis XVIII.
Adoration of the Magi. Oil. 10 ft. 10 in. × 8 ft. 1 in. Drawing only.
From the Collection of Napoleon III.
Seven Half-Figures in various Costumes (?). 1527. Fragment.
Bought from Campana Collection, Rome, by Napoleon III.

GERMANY.
ALTENBURG, SAXONY, MUSEUM.
Nine Fragments of Polyptych. Oil.
From the Collection of the late Herr von Lindenau.
Four small panels with a Saint in each, and five parts of a Predella: 1. Christ on the Mount of Olives. 2. Flagellation. 3. Crucifixion. 4. Deposition. 5. Resurrection.
[Pg 133]
BERLIN, GALLERY.
Two Wings of Altar-piece. 1498. Oil. 4 ft. 8 in. × 2 ft. 5½ in. [No. 79.]
Painted for the church of S. Agostino, Siena, which was burnt down in 1655. Bought from the Solly Collection.
Pan as God of Natural Life and Master of Music. Oil on canvas. 6 ft. 5 in. × 8 ft. 6½ in. [No. 79 A .]
Probably painted for Lorenzo dei Medici. Discovered in 1865 in the Palazzo Corsi, Florence. Bought by the Berlin Gallery 1873.
Inscribed: LVCA CORTONEN.
Holy Family. Oil. 10 in. × 10 in. Tondo. [No. 79 B .]
From the Patrizi Collection, Rome. Bought 1875.
Inscribed: LVCHAS SIGNORELLVS DE CORTONA.
Portrait of Man. Oil. 1 ft. 7 in. × 1 ft.
From the Torrigiani Collection, Florence.
MEININGEN, DUCAL PALACE.
Part of Predella.
MUNICH, GALLERY.
Madonna and Child. Oil. Tondo.
From the Palazzo Ginori, Florence.

ITALY.
ARCEVIA, S. MEDARDO (between Fabriano and Sinigalia).
Polyptych. Madonna and Saints. 1507. Oil. 8 ft. 8 in. × 8 ft. 8 in.
In the original Gothic frame. Inscribed: LVCAS SIGNORELLVS PINGEBAT. M.D.VII.
Predella : 1. The Annunciation. 2. The Nativity. 3. The Adoration of the Magi. 4. The Flight into Egypt. 5. The Murder of the Innocents.
[Pg 134]
ARCEVIA, S. MEDARDO, CAPPELLA DEL SACRAMENTO.
Baptism. 1508. Oil. 4 ft. 4 in. × 4 ft. 4 in.
In the original Gothic frame. Partly by assistants.
Predella : 1. The Birth of the Baptist. 2. The Preaching in the Desert. 3. The Denouncing of Herod and Herodias. 4. The Feast of Herod. 5. The Decapitation in Prison.
AREZZO, GALLERY.
Madonna, Saints, and Prophets. 1519. Oil. 11 ft. 7½ in. × 7 ft. 9 in. [No. 31.]
Painted for the Campagnia of San Girolamo. For many years in S. Croce; on the suppression of that convent in 1849 removed to S. Spirito; from thence to the Gallery.
AREZZO, DUOMO, SACRISTY.
Three Parts of Predella. Oil.
1. Birth of the Virgin. 2. Presentation. 3. Marriage of the Virgin.
BERGAMO, MORELLI COLLECTION.
S. Rock. Oil. [No. 19.]
Madonna. Oil. [No. 20.]
S. Sebastian. [No. 24.]
BORGO SAN SEPOLCRO, MUNICIPIO.
Church Standard. Oil on canvas. 6 ft. 4 in. × 4 ft. 6 in.
On one side a Crucifixion; on the other, SS. Antonio and Eligio.
From the Confraternity of S. Antonio Abbate.
CASTIGLIONE FIORENTINO COLLEGIATA, CAPPELLA DEL SACRAMENTO.
Deposition. Fresco. 8 ft. 10 in. × 8 ft. 10 in.
CITTÀ DI CASTELLO, GALLERY.
Martyrdom of S. Sebastian. 1496. Oil, 9 ft. 4 in. × 5 ft. 9½ in. [No. 19.]
From the church of S. Domenico.
[Pg 135]
CITTÀ DI CASTELLO, PALAZZO MANCINI.
Madonna and Saints. 1515. Oil.
Painted for the church of S. Francesco in Montone, near Umbertide. Discovered in a cellar in Montone.
Inscribed: EGREGIVM QVOD CERNIS OPVS MAGISTER ALOYSIUS EX GALLIA, ET TOMASINA EJVS VXOR EX DEVOTIONE SVIS SVMPTIBVS PONI CVRAVERVNT. LVCA SIGNORELLO DE CORTONA PICTORE INSIGNI FORMAS INDVCENTE. ANNO D. MDXV.
CORTONA, DUOMO.
Deposition. 1502. Oil. 8 ft. 10 in. × 8 ft 10 in.
From the church of Santa Margherita.
Inscribed (under frame): LVCAS AEGIDI SIGNORELLI. CORTONENSIS. MDII.
Predella to the Above :
1. Christ in Gethsemane. 2. The Last Supper. 3. The Betrayal. 4. The Flagellation.
The Institution of the Eucharist. 1512. Oil. 8 ft. 2 in. × 8 ft. 2 in.
From the high altar of the Gesù.
Inscribed:
LVCAS SIGNORELLIVS CORTHONIENSIS PINGEBAT. MDXII.
Conception of the Virgin. Oil.
The upper part the work of assistants.
CORTONA, S. DOMENICO (3rd altar, R.).
Madonna and Saints. 1515. Oil.
Painted for the Bishop of Cortona.
Inscribed: IO SERNINIVS EP̃S CORTONEÑS ICONAM ET ORNATUM P. P. FACIERI A.D. CI I XV. HAEREDES VERO D. ASTRVBALIS EJVS EX FV̆E AB NEPOTIS P. S. INSTAVRAN. CVRAVERVNT. A.D. CI . I . CXIX.
CORTONA, GESU.

Madonna and Saints.
[Pg 136]
CORTONA, S. NICCOLO.
Dead Christ upheld by Angels. Oil. 5 ft. ½ in. × 5 ft. 8½ in. On the Reverse—
Madonna Enthroned Between SS. Peter and Paul.
CORTONA, S. NICCOLO (on the wall, l. of entrance).
Madonna and Saints. Fresco. 9 ft. 4 in. × 9 ft. 8 in.
Discovered in 1847 by Don Agramante Lorini.
FLORENCE, ACADEMY.
Crucifixion. Oil, on canvas. [No. 6.] (Part of the design only.)
Madonna and Saints. Oil. [No. 54.]
From the church of S. Trinità, Cortona.
Predella. [No. 54.]
1. The Last Supper. 2. Christ in Gethsemane. 3. The Flagellation.
FLORENCE, CORSINI GALLERY.
Madonna and Saints. Tondo.
FLORENCE, PITTI.
Holy Family. Oil. 2 ft. 11 in. × 2 ft 11 in. Tondo. [No. 355.]
FLORENCE, UFFIZI.
Madonna and Child (1st Corridor). [No. 74.]
Probably painted for Lorenzo dei Medici. Later in the Villa of Duke Cosimo at Castello. Removed to the Gallery 1779.
Holy Family. Tondo. [No. 1291.]
Originally in the "Audienza dei Capitani," later in the "Stanza del Provveditore."
Predella. [No. 1298.]
1. The Annunciation. 2. The Nativity. 3. The Adoration of the Magi.
From the church of Santa Lucia, Montepulciano.
[Pg 137]
FOIANO (near Sinalunga), COLLEGIATA.
Coronation of the Virgin. 1523. Oil. 6 ft. 11 in. × 5 ft. 7 in.
Predella. (Two scenes only by Signorelli.)
LORETO, CHURCH OF THE SANTA CASA.
Frescoes. Probably finished before 1484.
(Left Sacristy) "Della Cura." (In the cupola) Angels, Evangelists, and Fathers of the Church. (Walls) Apostles, Incredulity of S. Thomas. (Over door) Conversion of Saul. (Nave) Medallions in *grisaille* of Prophets and Fathers of the Church.
MILAN, BRERA.
Madonna and Saints. 1508. Oil. 8 ft. 2 in. × 6 ft. 2½ in. [No. 197 bis .]
From the church of S. Francesco, Arcevia. First brought to the Gallery 1811. In 1815 removed to the church at Figino, near Milan. Replaced in the Gallery 1892.
Inscribed: LVCAS SIGNORELLI P. CORTONA (on the back of the throne), IACOBI SIMONIS PHILIPPINIS AERE DEO ET DIVÆ MARIAE DICATVM FR: BERNARDINO VIGNATO GVARDIANO PROCVRANTE. MDVIII.

The Flagellation. [No. 262.] { Probably one panel originally. 2 ft. 8½ in. × 2 ft.
Madonna and Child. [No. 281.]
From the church of Santa Maria del Mercato, Fabriano.
"The Flagellation" inscribed: OPVS LVCE CORTONENSIS.
MONTE OLIVETO (near Asciano), CLOISTERS.
Frescoes. 1497.
Eight scenes from the life of S. Benedict.
MORRA (near Città di Castello), S. CRESCENZIANO.
Crucifixion. Fresco.
Flagellation. Fresco.
[Pg 138]
ORVIETO, CATHEDRAL, CHAPEL OF THE MADONNA DI S. BRIZIO, FORMERLY CAPPELLA NUOVA.
Frescoes. 1499-1504.
(Six compartments in Vaulting): 1. Apostles; 2. Signs of the Passion; 3. Martyrs (design of Fra Angelico); 4. Virgins; 5. Patriarchs; 6. Fathers of the Church. (Four large frescoes): 1. Antichrist; 2. Crowning of the Elect; 3. Damnation; 4. Resurrection. (Window Wall): R. Hell; L. Heaven. (Round the Portal): Signs of Destruction. (Lower Walls): Pietà; Portraits of Poets; Medallions in *grisaille*.
ORVIETO, OPERA DEL DUOMO.
S. Maria Maddalena. 1504. Oil. 5 ft. 11 in. × 3 ft. 11 in.
Originally painted for the Cathedral.
Inscribed on the upper part of the frame:
CECCARELLEVS. DE. APVIDVTIS—ET RVFINVS ANTONII.—
On the lower:
CONSERVAT. PA. PACIS. CONSERVATRICI. EX. SE CONSVLTO. M.D.IIII.
Portraits of Signorelli and Niccolò Franceschi. [No. 1504.] Tempera on brick. 1 ft. × 1 ft. 3½ in.
Inscribed on the draperies: LVCA and NICOLAVS .
On the back, probably by Signorelli at the request of Niccolò Franceschi, the Treasurer of the Works:
LVCAS SIGNORELLVS. NATIONE YTALYS. PATRIA CORTONÊSIS. ARTE PICTVRE EXIMIVS. MERITO APELLI CONPARÂDVS. SVB REGIMINE ET STIPENDIO NICOLAI FRÃCH. EIVSDÊ NATIONIS PATRIE VRBEVETANE. CAMERARII FABRICE. HVIVS BASYLICE SACELLV̆ HOC VIRGINI DICATV̆ IVDICII FINALIS ORDINE FIGVRADV̆ PSPICVE PINSIT CVPIDVSQ ÎMORTALITATIS VTRIVSQ EFFIGIÊ ATFRGO LITTERARV̆ HARV̆ NATVRALITER MIRA EFFÎSIT ARTE. ALEXANDRO . VI° . PON . MAX . SEDENTE . ET MAXIMIANO. IIII . INPERIANTE AÑO SALVTIS MᶜCCCCC°. TEŘIO KALENDAS JANVARIAS.
[Pg 139]
PERUGIA, DUOMO, WINTER CHAPEL.
Madonna and Saints. 1484. Oil. 6 ft. 8 in. × 6 ft. 1½ in.
Inscribed (hidden by the frame):
JACOBVS VANNVTIVS NOBILIS CORTONENSIS OLIM EPISCOPVS PERVSINVS HOC DEO MAX. ET DIVO HONOPHRIO SACELLVM DEDICAVIT: CVI IN ARCHIEPISCOPVM NICAENVM ASSVMPTO NEPOS DIONISIVS SVCCESSIT, ET QVANTA VIDES IMPENSA ORNAVIT AE-

QVA PIETAS. M. CCCC. LXXXIV. ROME, ROSPIGLIOSI COLLECTION.

Holy Family. Oil. 2 ft. 8 in. × 2 ft. [Sala II., No. 3.]

UMBERTIDE, SANTA CROCE.

Deposition. Oil. 6 ft. 6 in. × 4 ft. 10 in.

Predella : 1. March of Constantine. 2. Discovery of the Cross. 3. Entry of Heraclius into Jerusalem.

URBINO, SANTA SPIRITO.

Church Standard . (Now divided.) Oil on canvas. 5 ft. × 3 ft. (On one side, Crucifixion ; on the other, Descent of the Holy Ghost at Pentecost .)

VOLTERRA, DUOMO, SACRISTY.

Annunciation. 1491. Oil.

Inscribed: LVCAS CORTONEN PINXIT MXDI.

A later inscription records its restoration in 1731.

VOLTERRA, MUNICIPIO.

Madonna and Saints. 1491. Oil.

From the church of S. Francesco.

Inscribed: MARIA. VERGINI. PETRVS. BELLADOMNA. HVJVS. RELIGIONIS PROFESSOR POS. LVCAS CORTONEÑ PINXIT. M CCCC LXXXXI.

[Pg 140]

VOLTERRA (first landing of stairs), MUNICIPIO.

S. Girolamo. Fresco.

UNITED STATES OF AMERICA.

NEW HAVEN. COLLECTION OF Mr JARVIS.

Part of Predella. Adoration of the Magi. Oil.

FOOTNOTES:

[94] The paintings, except when otherwise indicated, are on wood.
[Pg 141]

INDEX

Adoration of the Magi, The (Louvre), 37 ;
  (Arcevia), 93 ;
  (New Haven), 95
Agony in the Garden, The, 88
Ahasuerus and Esther, 103
Annunciation, The (Volterra), 7 , 49 , 50 ;
  (Uffizi), 50 ;
  (formerly Mancini collection), 51 ;
  (Arcevia), 93 , 94
Arcevia, Altar-piece at, 11 , 92
Baptism, The (Arcevia), 93
Berensen, B., 6 , 112
Bernabei, Tommaso, 115
Betrayal, The (Florence), 23 , 88 ;
  (Cortona), 23 , 88
Bicchi Family, Altar-piece for, 8 , 59
Birth of the Baptist, The (Arcevia), 95
Birth of the Virgin, The (Arezzo), 96
Bode, Dr, 43
Botticelli, 6 ;
  his "Calumny," 19 ;
  passion for swift movement, 23
Bramante, 11
Caporali, Giambattista, 11
Castagno, Andrea di, 19 ;
  influence of on Signorelli, 21
Christ in Gethsemane, 88
Circumcision, The, 38 , 39 , 47
Città di Castello, Frescoes at, 4 , 5 , 53 ;
  citizenship of presented to Signorelli, 7
Conception of the Virgin, The, 103
Conversion of Saul, The, 24 , 30 , 36
Coronation of the Virgin, The, 105
Cortona, Signorelli born at, 2 ;
  municipal appointments at, 5 , 6 , 8 , 10 ;
  the "Deposition" in the Cathedral of, 10 , 87
Crowe and Cavalcaselle, 6 , 21 , 37 , 39 , 83 , 113 , 118
Crowning of the Elect, The, 24 , 29 , 42 , 73
Crucifixion, The (Urbino), 52 ;
  (Borgo San Sepolcro), 61 , 88 ;
  (Morra), 61 , 104
Damnation, The, 8 , 22 , 76
Dante, Portraits of, by Signorelli, at Orvieto, 71 , 74 ;
  scenes from the Divina Commedia, 74 , 75
Dead Christ supported by Angels, 26 , 91
Death of Lucretia, Study for a, 109
Death of Moses, The, 6 , 112
Decapitation in Prison, The, 95
Denouncing of Herod and Herodias, 95
Deposition, The (Cortona), 10 , 87 ;
  (Umbertide), 14 , 22 , 100
Descent of the Holy Ghost, The, 52 , 53
Discovery of the Cross, The, 101
Dispute by the Way, The, 51
Donatello, his influence on Signorelli, 3 , 19 ;
  mastery of combined movement, 23
Entry of Heraclius into Jerusalem, The, 101
Feast of Herod, The, 95
Feast in the House of Simon, The, 52
Flagellation, The (Brera), 1 , 3 , 22 , 24 , 25 , 26 , 27 , 32 ;
  (Cortona), 88 ;
  (Florence), 88 ;
  (Morra), 27 , 104
Flight into Egypt, The, 93
Foiano, Altar-piece at, 16 , 105
[Pg 142] Foligno, Niccolò da, 95
Forlì, Melozzo da, 3
Fra Angelico, frescoes at Orvieto, 8 , 64 , 65 , 69
Franceschi, Pier dei, Signorelli the pupil of, 2 , 3 , 11 , 17 , 50 ;
  and Signorelli compared, 17 , 18 ;
  his "Death of Adam," 32 ;
  his "Resurrection," 61 ;
  his "Baptism," 94
Francesco, Niccolò, Portrait of, by Signorelli, 9 , 83 , 85
Gatta, Bartolommeo della, 6 , 35 ;
  an imitator of Signorelli, 111 , 112 , 113
Genga, Girolamo, 9 ;
  an imitator of Signorelli, 111 , 113
Gozzoli, Benozzo, 8 , 66 , 69
Guidobaldo, of Urbino, 9
Hercules overcoming Antæus (chalk drawing), 109
Holy Family (Rospigliosi Collection), 27 , 30 , 46 ;
  (Pitti), 38 , 45 ;
  (Uffizi), 26 , 47
Homer, Scenes from, at Orvieto, 72
Institution of the Eucharist, The, 95
Journey of Moses and Zipporah, The, fresco by Pintorricchio, 6
Last Judgment, The, 8 , 22 , 76
Last Supper, The (Cortona), 88 ;
  (Florence), 88
Lazzaro de' Taldi, Signorelli's uncle, 2
Lorenzo, Fiorenzo di, Reminiscences of, in Signorelli's work, 21

Loreto, Frescoes at, 5, 24, 29, 34
Lucan, Scenes from, at Orvieto, 81, 82
Luzi, Ludovico, "il Duomo di Orvieto," 69, 72, 74, 78, 81, 83
Madonna and Saints (Brera), 1, 29, 32, 99;
  (Volterra), 7, 29, 35, 49;
  (Arezzo), 14;
  (Uffizi), 28, 37, 41, 43;
  (Munich), 28, 41, 44;
  (Florence Academy), 29, 35, 89;
  (Corsini Gallery), 46;
  (Città di Castello), 24, 98;
  (S. Niccolò, Cortona), 91, 92;
  (S. Domenico, Cortona), 100
Magdalen, The, altar-piece (Orvieto), 85, 88
Mancini, Giacomo, 5, 99
Mancini, Girolamo, 5
March of Constantine, The, 101
Marriage of the Virgin, The, 96
Medici, Giovanni dei (Pope Leo X.), 12
Medici, Lorenzo dei, 4;
  friendship with Signorelli, 12, 41, 43
Michelangelo, Story of his dealings with Signorelli, 13
Milanesi, Signor, 89, 112
Missaghi, Guiseppe, 37
Monte Oliveto, Frescoes in the Benedictine Cloister at, 7, 22, 54, 63
Morelli, on the frescoes in the Sistine Chapel, 6;
  on Signorelli, 30, 61, 63;
  on his drawing, 107, 109;
  on his influence, 111;
  on Girolamo Genga, 114
Murder of the Innocents, The, 93
Nativity, The (Arcevia), 93;
  (Cortona), 96
Nude, Early treatment of the, 32
Orvieto, Frescoes in the Cathedral of, 8, 9, 29, 42, 58, 63 *et seq.*
Ovid, Scenes from, at Orvieto, 78
Pan, 28, 41, 42
Parens, Pietro, 80, 81
Perugia, Altar-piece in the Cathedral of, 7, 28, 38
Perugino, 6, 8, 11, 20, 66;
  his influence on Signorelli, 20, 37, 72
Pietà (Orvieto), 80
Pintorricchio, 6, 11;

frescoes in the Sistine Chapel by, 6; [Pg 143] asserted influence of, on Signorelli, 21
Pollaiuolo, Antonio, his influence on Signorelli, 3, 4, 18, 22, 37, 42, 50, 62, 94, 109;
  his "S. Sebastian," 18;
  his "Battle of the Nudes," 18, 22, 32;
  "Hercules," 18, 32
Portrait of a Man (Berlin), 45
Preaching and Fall of Antichrist, The, 70
Preaching in the Desert, The, 95
Presentation, The, 96
Quercia, Jacopo della, 60
Raffaelle, 11, 12, 114
Rain of Fire, The, 82
Resurrection, The, 79
Rome, Frescoes in the Sistine Chapel, 6;
  decoration of the Vatican chambers, 11
Rosselli, Cosimo, 6
Rumohr, on Signorelli, 21
S. Augustine, Scenes from the Life of, 103
S. Benedict, Scenes from the Life of, 54
S. Jerome, 7, 49
S. Martin, Scenes from the Life of, 106
S. Sebastian, The Martyrdom of, 53
Scalza, Ippolito, 80, 82
Signorelli, Antonio, 10, 115
Signorelli, Francesco, 115
Signorelli, Luca, little known of his life, 1;
  Vasari on, 1;
  birth, 2;
  studied painting under Pier dei Franceschi, 2;
  influence of Antonio Pollaiuolo and Donatello, 3, 4;
  gap in his biography, 4;
  early frescoes, 5;
  municipal appointments at Cortona, 5, 6, 8, 10, 16;
  his social status, 5;
  supposed visit to Rome, 6;
  frescoes in the Sistine Chapel ascribed to, 6;
  painted the altar-piece in Perugia Cathedral, 7;
  received the honour of citizenship

from Città di Castello, 7;
  pictures at Volterra, 7;
  frescoes in the cloister at Monte Oliveto, 7;
  altar-piece at Siena, 8;
  frescoes in the Cathedral of Orvieto, 8, 9;
  portraits of himself, 8, 9, 71, 85;
  the "Deposition" at Cortona, 10;
  death of his son Antonio, 10;
  and of Polidoro, 10;
  pictures at Arcevia, 11;
  decoration of the Vatican chambers, 11;
  disappointments at Rome, 12;
  alleged transaction with Michelangelo, 13;
  visit to Arezzo, 14, 15;
  death, 15;
  Vasari's character of, 16;
  artists who influenced, 17, 20;
  origin of the swaggering posture so characteristic of his paintings, 19, 20;
  use of gold and gesso, 21, 29;
  his great achievement, the rendering of combined action, 22;
  his defects, 24, 25;
  his colour, 25;
  his line and modelling, 26;
  an unequal illustrator, 26, 27;
  his painting of children, 27;
  realism, 28;
  repetitions, 29;
  chief qualities of his work, 29;
  earliest works, 32;
  frescoes at Loreto, 34;
  altar-piece at Perugia, 38;
  qualities of his *Tondos*, 47;
  works at Volterra, 49;
  frescoes at Monte Oliveto, 54;
  the Orvieto frescoes, 63, 86;
  later works, 87;
  altar-piece at Arcevia, 92;
  last works, 98, 106;
  drawings, 107, 110;
  his imitators and influence, 111, 119
Signorelli, Pier Tommaso, 15, 115
Signorelli, Polidoro, 9, 115;
  his death, 10
Signs of the Destruction of the World, 82
Sodoma, 8, 11, 40, 59
Standards painted by Signorelli, 7, 52, 61
Supper at Emmaus, The, 51

[Pg 144] Uccello, Paolo, 18
Van der Goes, Hugo, 39
Vasari, on Signorelli, 1 , 3 , 11 , 13 , 14 , 15 , 16 , 35 , 38 , 40 , 54 , 59 , 60 , 64 , 87 , 95 , 96 , 102 , 113
Verrocchio, Reminiscences of, in Signorelli's work, 21 , 36
Vischer, on the frescoes in the Sistine Chapel, 6 ;
on Signorelli, 21 , 35 , 36 , 39 , 92 ;
list of Signorelli's drawings, 110
Visitation, The, 60
Way to Calvary, The, 88
Zaccagna, Turpino, 116

W. H. WHITE AND CO. LTD., RIVERSIDE PRESS, EDINBURGH
NOTICE
P HOTOGRAPHS of most of the works mentioned in this volume are to be obtained in various sizes from
W. A. MANSELL & Co.
Art Photograph Publishers and Dealers,
405, OXFORD STREET,
LONDON, W.
16, PALL MALL EAST, S.W.
Permanent Carbon Points, Permanent Prints, Photogravures, from most of the Pictures in the

Galleries
AT
LONDON.   MILAN.   VIENNA
National   VENICE.   Liechten
Gallery.   MUNICH.   Belveder
Dulwich   BERLIN.   Czernin.
Gallery.   DRESDEN.   AMSTE

Tate Gallery.
EDINBURGH.
GLASGOW.
BRUSSELS.
Etc., Etc.
Royal Collections
AT
BUCKINGHAM PALACE.
WINDSOR CASTLE.
Private Collections
OF
The Duke of Devonshire.
The Earl Spencer.
The Earl of Northbrook.
ART BOOKS—ART ALBUMS—ARTISTIC FRAMING.
FRANZ HANFSTÆNGL
16, PALL MALL EAST, S.W.
Lists and Prospectuses Free.
Catalogues, One Shilling.
FINE ART ENGRAVERS
AND PRINTERS.
THE
SWAN ELECTRIC
ENGRAVING
COMPANY,
116, Charing Cross Road, London, W.C.
ENGRAVERS AND PRINTERS
OF PHOTOGRAVURE PLATES.
OF "SWANTYPE" BLOCKS.
OF FINE LINE-WORK.
THE LEADING FIRM IN GREAT BRITAIN FOR
ALL HIGH-CLASS REPRODUCTION WORK,

Hague, F
lem.
CASSEL

INCLUDING THE ORTHOCHROMATIC
PHOTOGRAPHY OF PICTURES AND WORKS OF ART.

TRANSCRIBERS' NOTES

General: Corrections to punctuation have not been individually noted.

Page xii: Erratum applied to text.

Page xiii: GUIDÀ corrected to GUIDA. RELLA corrected to NELLA.

Page 64: "By the which he roused" amended to "By means of this he roused".

Page 72: Duplicate a removed from "In that on the left a a man".

Page 94: ninteen corrected to nineteen.

Page 102: Campagnia standardised to Compagnia.

Page 108: Pietá corrected to Pietà.

Page 135: Unicode character X2183 (Roman Numeral Reversed One Hundred) is not supported in all fonts.

Page 138: PSPICVE without tilde as in original, probably intended as an abbreviation for PERSPICUE. FIGVRADV̆ as in original, perhaps a misspelling of FIGURANDUM. ATFRGO as in original perhaps intended A TERGO. CVPIDVSQ (Cupidusque?) and VTRIVSQ (Utriusque?) as in original without overlining.

***